101 poems about childhood

# 101 POEMS ABOUT CHILDHOOD

*also by Michael Donaghy*

*poetry*
SHIBBOLETH
ERRATA
DANCES LEARNED LAST NIGHT: POEMS 1975–1995
CONJURE
SAFEST

*prose*
WALLFLOWERS: A Lecture on Poetry

# 101 POEMS
# ABOUT CHILDHOOD

*edited by*
MICHAEL DONAGHY

*faber and faber*

First published in 2005
by Faber and Faber Limited
3 Queen Square London WC1N 3AU

Photoset by Refinecatch Ltd, Bungay, Suffolk
Printed in England by Mackays of Chatham plc, Chatham, Kent

The right of the Estate of Michael Donaghy to be identified as editor
of this work has been asserted in accordance with Section 77
of the Copyright, Designs and Patents Act 1988

A CIP record for this book
is available from the British Library

ISBN 0-571-21784-2

2 4 6 8 10 9 7 5 3 1

# Contents

[ VIII ]

# Storm the Earth and Stun the Air

There's an assumption abroad nowadays that poetry and childhood are naturally linked, that if you write poetry you must perforce also write children's poetry or be charmingly or sadly childlike yourself. And poets are expected to be obsessed with recording the details of their early years, rehearsing their gauzy raptures or picking at the scabs of abuse. I'm sure there are sound, boring reasons for all this involving the economics of publishing and the clichés of journalism, but I think poetry and childhood may be entwined on a deeper level. We first encounter poems in the form of nursery rhymes. We learn much of our language through verse, and, largely due to the resistance and exclusivity of contemporary serious poetry, many adults today only encounter poems as something they read to their kids at bedtime, kids who will soon enter into their own verse culture of rude playground chants, skipping rhymes and taunts and who will, a few years later, learn rock lyrics and rap by heart.

In one sense, all poetry is kids' stuff. What makes us recognise a piece of writing as a poem is often a 'technique' whereby poets imitate children's thinking. Rhyme and rhythm, of course, are the very stuff of the nursery rhymes and dandling songs with which cultures the world over prompt their children toward speech. But even those more sophisticated and 'literary' effects we learn to recognise and name in school have their roots in childhood. When Baudelaire, for example, writes that some perfumes are as sweet as the sound of an oboe or fresh as a child's embrace, we say he's using a technique called *synaesthesia* whereby a sensation in one sense triggers an image or sensation in another. But some psychologists hold that we all experience sensation in this undifferentiated way up to about four months of age. When Rilke tells us that a headless statue looks at us, or Elizabeth Bishop tells us that a knife will not look at her, we say they're employing *personification*, but a substantial school of psychoanalysis traces all such metaphors back to the crib, to that 'special' blanket or teddy bear, the 'transitional object' by which toddlers negotiate separation from their mothers. When Wordsworth describes the earth 'Apparelled in celestial light/ The glory and the freshness of a dream', or when Traherne claims to have beheld in his angel infancy the shadows of eternity in clouds and flowers, we know they're not just framing theological arguments, but reporting early experiences of startling clarity. Some neurologists argue that as infants our consciousness is extraordinarily intense and receptive and that during this period we're terribly vulnerable, requiring longer periods of parenting than any other animal. They argue that language delimits that consciousness to manageable chunks, a powerful evolutionary advantage, like an opposable thumb. Only occasionally, they argue, are adults permitted to return to that awe-struck state before we framed the world in words. Perhaps poetry is our way of using the power of language against itself so that, however briefly, we see and feel the world afresh, with all the intensity of infancy. What about abstract thought, I hear you ask? After all, we expect wisdom from poets, as we expect it from philosophers and cosmologists. In fact, we expect them all to pose the very same questions children ask: What is *is*? Why is there anything? And why doesn't it all happen at once? Like children's art, children's speculative thought shows a resourcefulness and curiosity missing from most adults.

So you might say every poem invokes childhood on some level. But I had to be somewhat particular in choosing a mere 101 for this anthology. Be advised: this is not a book of children's poetry. Much of it is challenging and some of it bleak. There are dead children here, but it's not a collection of elegies. And while I couldn't resist some ecstatic observations of children by parents and poems of parental love, remorse and responsibility, it's not really a book about parenthood either. Some great names are missing, and readers will wonder why I haven't included such classics as 'Among School Children' or 'Prayer for My Daughter' (both poems depart from childhood pretty rapidly). And many of my contemporaries will wonder why I've passed over their work (sorry, but you've *all* written poems about childhood and you're outnumbered by the dead). I was most interested in poems about children's minds. These seemed to fall into three categories: either a descriptive observation of a child by an adult spectator (Pinsky, Baille, Williams, Rilke), a rhetorical poem discoursing on that state of mind and the development of our language and emotions (see Graves, Burnside, Duffy) or a directly recalled or imaginary event dramatising the energy with which children encounter the world (see Bishop, Jarrell, Justice).

I resisted the impulse to show off by making clever connections through time and decided instead to play the historian, ordering the poems chronologically to illustrate the development of childhood through the ages. Of course, it wound up fairly distorted. There's a gap of about two thousand years between the first and second items, for one thing, and I've included so few poems in translation readers may wonder why I bothered. Childhood, as distinct from children, didn't really exist before the seventeenth century and poets rarely considered children except to mourn their deaths, yet I've given Traherne and Vaughan more than their fair share in order to mark the invention of childhood and the developing idea of childhood spirituality. There are plenty of nineteenth-century poems condemning child labour, but most of them aren't any good. So I let Blake, Browning and Meynell represent that line. And I've omitted the deluge of mawkish Victoriana, though you can spot shadings of it in Hood and Swinburne. The disproportionate number of twentieth-century poems in these pages reflects the rise of psychoanalysis and the increasing conviction that childhood holds the key to what we are. As Adam Phillips says, with the invention of childhood comes a new kind of person, one with a private inner world. So it's not surprising that the growth in poems about children and childhood parallels the decline of public poetry and the expectation that a poet speaks for and to the public. The poetry of childhood also fills the gap left by the decline of religious poetry. Where poets of previous centuries were principally concerned with where their souls were headed, twentieth century poets are far more concerned with where they came from. Where Traherne and Vaughan only looked back to their innocence to catch a glimpse of the heaven from whence it issued, modern poets look back to childhood itself as the source of all meaning.

I'd like to thank all my friends who offered suggestions including Eva Salzman, Anne Rouse, William Thomson, Bill Wenthe, Dan Tobin, Bill Swainson and Sean O'Brien. But mostly I want to thank Maddy, my wife and collaborator, whose idea this was, and Ruairi, my son, for patiently remaining a child for the duration of the project.

Michael Donaghy

# 101 POEMS ABOUT CHILDHOOD

# from *The Iliad*, Book VI

As he said this, Hector held out his arms
to take his baby. But the child squirmed round
on the nurse's bosom and began to wail,
terrified by his father's great war helm –
the flashing bronze, the crest with horsehair plume
tossed like a living thing at every nod.
His father began laughing, and his mother
laughed as well. Then from his handsome head
Hector lifted off his helm and bent
to place it, bright with sunlight, on the ground.
    When he had kissed his child and swung him high
to dandle him, he said this prayer: 'O Zeus
and all immortals, may this child, my son,
become like me a prince among the Trojans.
Let him be strong and brave and rule in power
at Ilium; then someday men will say
"This fellow is far better than his father!"
seeing him home from war, and in his arms
the bloodstained gear of some tall warrior slain –
making his mother proud.'

                         After this prayer,
into his dear wife's arms he gave his baby,
whom on her fragrant breast
she held and cherished, laughing through her tears.

*translated from the Greek by Robert Fitzgerald*

# When We Were Children

I remember how, at that time, in this meadow,
We used to run up and down, playing our games,
Tag and games of that sort; and looked for wildflowers,
Violets and such. A long time ago.
Now there are only these cows, bothered by flies,
Only these cows, wandering about in the meadow.

I remember us sitting down in the field of flowers,
Surrounded by flowers, and playing she loves me not,
She loves me; plucking the flower petals.
My memory of childhood is full of those flowers,
Bright with the colors of garlands we wore in our dancing
And playing. So time went by among the wildflowers.

Look over there near those trees at the edge of the woods.
Right over there is where we used to find
Blueberry bushes, blackberry bushes, wild strawberries.
We had to climb over rocks and old walls to get them.
One day a man called out to us: 'Children, go home.'
He had been watching from somewhere in the woods.

We used to feast on the berries we found in that place
Till our hands and mouths were stained with the colors of all
The berries the blackberries, strawberries, and the
    blueberries.
It was all fun to us, in the days of our childhood.
One day a man called out, in a doleful voice:
'Go home, children, go home, there are snakes in that place.'

One day one of the children went into the grass
That grows high near the woods, among the bushes.

[4]

We heard him scream and cry out. He came back weeping.
'Our little horse is lying down and bleeding.
Our pony is lying down. Our pony is dying.
I saw a snake go crawling off in the grass.'

Children, go home, before it gets too dark.
If you don't go home before the light has gone,
If you don't get home before the night has come,
Listen to me, you will be lost in the dark,
Listen to me, your joy will turn into sorrow.
Children, go home, before it gets to be dark.

*There were five virgins lingered in the field.*
*The king went in with his bride and shut the doors.*
*The palace doors were shut against the virgins.*
*The virgins wept left standing in the field.*
*The servants came and stripped the virgins naked.*
*The virgins wept, stripped naked, in the field.*

*translated from the German by David Ferry*

## 'When Forty Winters Shall Besiege Thy Brow'

When forty winters shall besiege thy brow,
And dig deep trenches in thy beauty's field,
Thy youth's proud livery so gazed on now,
Will be a totter'd weed of small worth held:
Then being asked, where all thy beauty lies,
Where all the treasure of thy lusty days;
To say, within thine own deep sunken eyes,
Were an all-eating shame, and thriftless praise.
How much more praise deserv'd thy beauty's use,
If thou couldst answer 'This fair child of mine
Shall sum my count, and make my old excuse,'
Proving his beauty by succession thine!
    This were to be new made when thou art old,
    And see thy blood warm when thou feel'st it cold.

# from *The Winter's Tale*

POLIXENES

    We were, fair queen,
    Two lads that thought there was no more behind
    But such a day to-morrow as to-day,
    And to be boy eternal.

HERMIONE

    Was not my lord the verier wag o' the two?

POLIXENES

    We were as twinn'd lambs that did frisk i' the sun,
    And bleat the one at the other: what we chang'd
    Was innocence for innocence; we knew not
    The doctrine of ill-doing, nor dream'd
    That any did. Had we pursu'd that life,
    And our weak spirits ne'er been higher rear'd
    With stronger blood, we should have answer'd
      heaven
    Boldly 'not guilty'; the imposition clear'd
    Hereditary ours.

## De Puero Balbutiente

Methinks 'tis pretty sport to hear a child
Rocking a word in mouth yet undefiled;
The tender racquet rudely plays the sound
Which, weakly bandied, cannot back rebound;
And the soft air the softer roof doth kiss
With a sweet dying and a pretty miss,
Which hears no answer yet from the white rank
Of teeth not risen from their coral bank.
The alphabet is searched for letters soft
To try a word before it can be wrought;
And when it slideth forth, it goes as nice
As when a man doth walk upon the ice.

## On My First Son

Farewell, thou child of my right hand, and joy;
My sin was too much hope of thee, loved boy.
Seven years thou wert lent to me, and I thee pay,
Exacted by thy fate, on the just day.
Oh, could I lose all father, now! For why
Will man lament the state he should envy?
To have so soon scaped world's and flesh's rage,
And, if no other misery, yet age!
Rest in soft peace, and, asked, say here doth lie
Ben Jonson his best piece of poetry;
For whose sake, henceforth, all his vows be such,
As what he loves may never like too much.

# On My First Daughter

Here lies to each her parents' ruth,
Mary, the daughter of their youth:
Yet, all Heaven's gifts being heaven's due,
It makes the father less to rue.
At six months' end she parted hence
With safety of her innocence;
Whose soul heaven's queen (whose name she bears),
In comfort of her mother's tears,
Hath placed amongst her virgin train:
Where, while that severed doth remain,
This grave partakes the fleshly birth;
Which cover lightly, gentle earth.

# On The Infancy of Our Saviour

Hail blessed Virgin, full of heavenly Grace,
Blest above all that sprang from human race;
Whose Heav'n-saluted Womb brought forth in One,
A blessed Saviour, and a blessed Son:
O! What a ravishment 't had been, to see
Thy little Saviour perking on thy Knee!
To see him nuzzle in thy Virgin-Breast:
His milk-white body all unclad, undrest!
To see thy busie fingers cloathe and wrap
His spreading limbs in thy indulgent Lap!
To see his desp'rate Eyes, with Childish grace
Smiling upon his smiling Mother's face!
And when his forward strength began to bloom,
To see him diddle up and down the Room!
O, who would think so sweet a Babe as this,
Should e'er be slain by a false-hearted kisse!
Had I a Ragge, if sure thy Body wore it,
Pardon, sweet Babe, I think I should adore it:
Till then, O grant this Boon, (a boon or dearer)
The Weed not being, I may adore the Wearer.

GEORGE HERBERT (1593–1633)

## Holy Baptisme (II)

Since, Lord, to thee
A narrow way and little gate
Is all the passage, on my infancie
Thou didst lay hold, and antedate
My faith in me.

O let me still
Write thee great God, and me a childe:
Let me be soft and supple to thy will,
Small to myself, to others milde,
Behither ill.

Although by stealth
My flesh get on; yet let her sister
My soul bid nothing, but preserve her wealth:
The growth of flesh is but a blister;
Childhood is health.

# Of the Four Ages of Man: Childhood

Ah me! conceiv'd in sin and born with sorrow,
A nothing, here to day and gone to morrow,
Whose mean beginning blushing can't reveal,
But night and darkness must with shame conceal.
My mothers breeding sickness I will spare,
Her nine months weary burden not declare.
To shew her bearing pains, I should do wrong,
To tell those pangs which can't be told by tongue:
With tears into the world I did arrive,
My mother still did waste as I did thrive,
Who yet with love and all alacrity,
Spending, was willing to be spent for me.
With wayward cries I did disturb her rest,
Who sought still to appease me with the breast:
With weary arms she danc'd and *By By* sung,
When wretched I ingrate had done the wrong.
When infancy was past, my childishness
Did act all folly that it could express,
My silliness did only take delight
In that which riper age did scorn and slight.
In Rattles, Bables and such toyish stuff,
My then ambitious thoughts were low enough:
My high-born soul so straightly was confin'd,
That its own worth it did not know nor mind:
This little house of flesh did spacious count,
Through ignorance all troubles did surmount;
Yet this advantage had mine ignorance
Freedom from envy and from arrogance.
How to be rich or great I did not cark,

A Baron or a Duke ne'r made my mark,
Nor studious was Kings favours how to buy,
With costly presence or base flattery:
No office coveted wherein I might
Make strong my self and turn aside weak right:
No malice bare to this or that great Peer,
Nor unto buzzing whisperers gave ear:
I gave no hand nor vote for death or life,
I'd nought to do 'twixt King and peoples' strife.
No Statist I: nor Marti'list i' th' field,
Where ere I went mine innocence was shield.
My quarrels not for Diadems did rise,
But for an apple, plum, or some such prize:
My strokes did cause no blood no wounds or scars,
My little wrath did end soon as my wars:
My Duel was no challenge nor did seek
My foe should weltering in his bowels reek.
I had no suits at law neighbours to vex,
Nor evidence for lands did me perplex.
I fear'd no storms, nor all the wind that blows,
I had no ships at Sea; nor fraughts to loose.
I fear'd no drought nor wet, I had no crop,
Nor yet on future things did set my hope.
This was mine innocence, but oh the seeds
Lay raked up of all the cursed weeds
Which sprouted forth in mine ensuing age,
As he can tell that next comes on the stage:
But yet let me relate before I go
The sins and dangers I am subject to,
Stained from birth with Adam's sinful fact,
Thence I began to sin as soon as act:
A perverse will, a love to what's forbid,
A serpents sting in pleasing face lay hid:

A lying tongue as soon as it could speak,
And fifth Commandment do daily break.
Oft stubborn, peevish, sullen, pout and cry,
Then nought can please, and yet I know not why.
As many are my sins, so dangers too;
For sin brings sorrow, sickness death and woe:
And though I miss the tossings of the mind,
Yet griefs in my frail flesh I still do find.
What gripes of wind mine infancy did pain,
What tortures I in breeding teeth sustain?
What crudities my stomach cold hath bred,
Whence vomits, flux and worms have issued?
What breaches, knocks and falls I daily have,
And some perhaps I carry to my grave,
Sometimes in fire, sometimes in water fall,
Strangely presev'd, yet mind it not at all:
At home, abroad my dangers manifold,
That wonder 'tis, my glass till now doth hold.
I've done; unto my elders I give way,
For 'tis but little that a child can say.

# The Picture of Little T. C. in a Prospect of Flowers

See with what simplicity
This nymph begins her golden days!
In the green grass she loves to lie,
And there with her fair aspect tames
The wilder flowers, and gives them names;
But only with the roses plays,
And them does tell
What colour best becomes them, and what smell.

Who can foretell for what high cause
This darling of the gods was born?
Yet this is she whose chaster laws
The wanton love shall one day fear,
And, under her command severe,
See his bow broke and ensigns torn.
Happy, who can
Appease this virtuous enemy of man!

O then let me in time compound
And parley with those conquering eyes,
Ere they have tried their force to wound;
Ere, with their glancing wheels, they drive
In triumph over hearts that strive,
And them that yield but more despise:
Let me be laid,
Where I may see thy glories from some shade.

Meantime, whilst every verdant thing
Itself does at thy beauty charm,
Reform the errors of the Spring;

Make that the tulips may have share
Of sweetness, seeing they are fair,
 And Roses of their thorns disarm;
  But most procure
That violets may a longer age endure.

  But O, young beauty of the woods,
  Whom Nature courts with fruits and flowers,
  Gather the flowers, but spare the buds;
 Lest Flora angry at thy crime
 To kill her infants in their prime,
  Do quickly make th' example yours;
   And ere we see,
Nip in the blossom all our hopes and thee.

# Childhood

I cannot reach it; and my striving eye
Dazzles at it, as at eternity.
    Were now that chronicle alive,
Those white designs which children drive,
And the thoughts of each harmless hour,
With their content too in my power,
Quickly would I make my path even,
And by mere playing go to Heaven.

    Why should men love
A wolf, more than a lamb or dove?
Or choose hell-fire and brimstone streams
Before bright stars and God's own beams?
Who kisseth thorns will hurt his face,
But flowers do both refresh and grace;
And sweetly living (*fie on men!*)
Are, when dead, medicinal then;
If seeing much should make staid eyes,
And long experience should make wise;
Since all that age doth teach is ill,
Why should I not love child-hood still?
Why, if I see a rock or shelf,
Shall I from thence cast down myself?
Or by complying with the world,
From the same precipice be hurled?
Those observations are but foul,
Which make me wise to lose my soul.

And yet the *practice* worldlings call
Business, and weighty action all,

Checking the poor child for his play,
But gravely cast themselves away.

Dear, harmless age! the short, swift span,
Where weeping virtue parts with man;
Where love without lust dwells, and bends
What way we please without self-ends.

An age of mysteries! which he
Must live twice, that would God's face see;
Which *Angels* guard, and with it play:
Angels! which foul men drive away.

How do I study now, and scan
Thee, more than ere I studied man,
And only see through a long night
Thy edges and thy bordering light!
Oh for thy centre and mid-day!
For sure that is the *narrow way*.

# The Retreat

Happy those early days! when I
Shined in my Angel-infancy.
Before I understood this place
Appointed for my second race,
Or taught my soul to fancy ought
But a white, celestial thought;
When yet I had not walked above
A mile or two from my first love,
And looking back (at that short space,)
Could see a glimpse of his bright face;
When on some *gilded cloud*, or *flower*
My gazing soul would dwell an hour,
And in those weaker glories spy
Some shadows of eternity;
Before I taught my tongue to wound
My conscience with a sinful sound,
Or had the black art to dispense
A several sin to every sense,
But felt through all this fleshy dress
Bright *shoots* of everlastingness.

    Oh how I long to travel back
And tread again that ancient track!
That I might once more reach that plain
Where first I left my glorious train,
From whence the enlightened spirit sees
That shady City of palm trees;
But (ah!) my soul with too much stay
Is drunk, and staggers in the way!
Some men a forward motion love,

But I by backward steps would move;
And when this dust falls to the urn,
In that state I came return.

THOMAS TRAHERNE (1638–74)

# The Approach

### 1

That childish thoughts such joys inspire,
Doth make my wonder, and His glory higher,
His bounty, and my wealth more great
It chews His Kingdom, and His work complete.
In which there is not anything,
Not meet to be the joy of Cherubim.

### 2

He in our childhood with us walks,
And with our thoughts mysteriously He talks;
He often visiteth our minds,
But cold acceptance in us ever finds:
We send Him often grieved away,
Who else would show us all His Kingdom's joy.

### 3

O Lord, I wonder at Thy Love,
Which did my infancy so early move:
But more at that which did forbear
And move so long, though slighted many a year:
But most of all, at last that Thou
Thyself shouldst me convert, I scarce know how.

### 4

Thy gracious motions oft in vain
Assaulted me: my heart did hard remain
Long time: I sent my God away
Grieve'd much, that He could not give me His joy.
I careless was, nor did regard
The end for which He all those thoughts prepar'd.

5

    But now, with new and open eyes,
I see beneath, as if above the skies,
    And as I backward look again
See all His thoughts and mine most clear arid
    plain.
    He did approach, He me did woo;
I wonder that my God this thing would do,

6

    From nothing taken first, I was;
What wondrous things His glory brought to pass!
    Now in the World I Him behold,
And me, enveloped in precious gold;
    In deep abysses of delights,
In present hidden glorious benefits.

7

    Those thoughts His goodness long before
Prepared as precious and celestial store
    With curious art in me inlaid,
That childhood might itself alone be said
    My Tutor, Teacher, Guide to be,
Instructed then even by the Deity.

# Innocence

But that which most I wonder at, which most
I did esteem my bliss, which most I boast,
And ever shall enjoy, is that within
 I felt no stain, nor spot of sin.

 No darkness then did overshade,
 But all within was pure and bright,
 No guilt did crush, nor fear invade
 But all my soul was full of light.

 A joyful sense and purity
  Is all I can remember;
 The very night to me was bright,
 'Twas summer in December.

2

A serious meditation did employ
My soul within, which taken up with joy
Did seem no outward thing to note, but fly
 All objects that do feed the eye.

 While it those very objects did
 Admire, and prize, and praise, and love,
 Which in their glory most are hid,
 Which presence only doth remove.

 Their constant daily presence I
  Rejoicing at, did see;
 And that which takes them from the eye
 Of others, offered them to me.

3

No inward inclination did I feel
To avarice or pride: my soul did kneel
In admiration all the day. No lust, nor strife,
    Polluted then my infant life.

    No fraud nor anger in me moved,
    No malice, jealousy, or spite:
    All that I saw I truly loved.
    Contentment only and delight

    Were in my soul. O heaven! what bliss
        Did I enjoy and feel!
    What powerful delight did this
    Inspire! for this I daily kneel.

4

Whether it be that nature is so pure,
And custom only vicious; or that sure
God did by miracle the guilt remove,
    And make my soul to feel his love

    So early; or that 'twas one day,
    Wherein this happiness I found;
    Whose strength and brightness so do ray,
    That still it seems me to surround;

    Whate're it is, it is a light
        So endless unto me
    That I a world of true delight
    Did then and to this day do see.

5

That prospect was the gate of heaven, that day
The ancient light of Eden did convey

Into my soul: I was an Adam there
    A little Adam in a sphere

Of joys! O there my ravished sense
Was entertain'd in Paradise,
And had a sight of innocence
All was beyond all bound and price.

An antepast of heaven sure!
    I on the earth did reign;
Within, without me, all was pure;
I must become a child again.

# To a Child of Quality Five Years Old, the Author Supposed Forty

Lords, knights, and squires, the num'rous band
    That wear the fair Miss Mary's fetters,
Were summoned by her high command
    To show their passion by their letters.

My pen amongst the rest I took,
    Lest those bright eyes, that cannot read,
Should dart their kindling fires, and look
    The pow'r they have to be obeyed.

Nor quality, nor reputation,
    Forbid me yet my flame to tell;
Dear five years old befriends my passion,
    And I may write till she can spell.

For, while she makes her silkworms beds
    With all the tender things I swear;
Whilst all the house my passion reads,
    In papers round her baby's hair;

She may receive and own my flame,
    For, though the strictest prudes should know it,
She'll pass for a most virtuous dame,
    And I for an unhappy poet.

Then too, alas! when she shall tear
    The lines some younger rival sends,
She'll give me leave to write, I fear,
    And we shall still continue friends.

For, as our different ages move,
    'Tis so ordained (would Fate but mend it!)
That I shall be past making love
    When she begins to comprehend it.

AMBROSE PHILIPS (1674–1749)

## To Miss Charlotte Pulteney in Her Mother's Arms

Timely blossom, infant fair,
Fondling of a happy pair,
Every morn and every night,
Their solicitous delight,
Sleeping, waking, still at ease,
Pleasing, without skill to please,
Little gossip, blithe and hale,
Tattling many a broken tale,
Singing many a tuneless song,
Lavish of a heedless tongue,
Simple maiden, void of art,
Babbling out the very heart,
Yet abandoned to thy will,
Yet imagining no ill,
Yet too innocent to blush,
Like the linlet in the bush,
To the mother-linnet's note
Moduling her slender throat,
Chirping forth thy petty joys,
Wanton in the change of toys,
Like the linnet green in May,
Flitting to each bloomy spray,
Wearied then, and glad of rest,
Like the linlet in the nest.
This thy present happy lot,
This, in time, will be forgot:

Other pleasures, other cares,
Ever-busy time prepares;
And thou shalt in thy daughter see
This picture, once, resembled thee.

## THOMAS GRAY (1716–71)

# Ode on a Distant Prospect of Eton College

Ye distant spires, ye antique towers,
That crown the watery glade,
Where grateful Science still adores
Her Henry's holy shade;
And ye, that from the stately brow
Of Windsor's heights th' expanse below
Of grove, of lawn, of mead survey,
Whose turf, whose shade, whose flowers among
Wanders the hoary Thames along
His silver-winding way.

Ah happy hills, ah pleasing shade,
Ah fields beloved in vain,
Where once my careless childhood strayed,
A stranger yet to pain!
I feel the gales, that from ye blow,
A momentary bliss bestow,
As waving fresh their gladsome wing,
My weary soul they seem to soothe,
And, redolent of joy and youth,
To breathe a second spring.

Say, Father Thames, for thou hast seen
Full many a sprightly race
Disporting on thy margent green
The paths of pleasure trace,
Who foremost now delight to cleave
With pliant arm thy glassy wave?
The captive linnet which enthral?
What idle progeny succeed

To chase the rolling circle's speed,
Or urge the flying ball?

   While some on earnest business bent
Their murm'ring labours ply
'Gainst graver hours, that bring constraint
To sweeten liberty:
Some bold adventurers disdain
The limits of their little reign,
And unknown regions dare descry:
Still as they run they look behind,
They hear a voice in every wind,
And snatch a fearful joy.

   Gay hope is theirs by fancy fed,
Less pleasing when possest;
The tear forgot as soon as shed,
The sunshine of the breast:
Theirs buxom health of rosy hue,
Wild wit, invention ever-new,
And lively cheer of vigour born;
The thoughtless day, the easy night,
The spirits pure, the slumbers light,
That fly th' approach of morn.

   Alas! regardless of their doom,
The little victims play!
No sense have they of ills to come,
Nor care beyond today:
Yet see how all around 'em wait
The Ministers of human fate,
And black Misfortune's baleful train!
Ah, show them where in ambush stand
To seize their prey, the murd'rous band!
Ah, tell them they are men!

These shall the fury Passions tear,
The vultures of the mind,
Disdainful Anger, pallid Fear,
And Shame that skulks behind;
Or pining Love shall waste their youth,
Or Jealousy with rankling tooth,
That inly gnaws the secret heart,
And Envy wan, and faded Care,
Grim-visaged comfortless Despair,
And Sorrow's piercing dart.

Ambition this shall tempt to rise,
Then whirl the wretch from high,
To bitter Scorn a sacrifice,
And grinning Infamy.
The stings of Falsehood those shall try,
And hard Unkindness' altered eye,
That mocks the tear it forced to flow;
And keen Remorse with blood defiled,
And moody Madness laughing wild
Amid severest woe.

Lo, in the vale of years beneath
A grisly troop are seen,
The painful family of Death,
More hideous than their Queen:
This racks the joints, this fires the veins,
That every labouring sinew strains,
Those in the deeper vitals rage:
Lo, Poverty, to fill the band,
That numbs the soul with icy hand,
And slow-consuming Age.

To each his suff'rings: all are men,
Condemned alike to groan;
The tender for another's pain,
Th' unfeeling for his own.
Yet ah! why should they know their fate?
Since sorrow never comes too late,
And happiness too swiftly flies.
Thought would destroy their paradise.
No more; where ignorance is bliss,
'Tis folly to be wise.

WILLIAM BLAKE (1757–1827)

# Holy Thursday

Twas on a Holy Thursday their innocent faces clean
The children walking two & two in red & blue & green
Grey headed beadles walkd before with wands as white as
    snow
Till into the high dome of Paul's they like Thames waters
    flow

O what a multitude they seemd these flowers of London
    town
Seated in companies they sit with radiance all their own
The hum of multitudes was there but multitudes of lambs
Thousands of little boys & girls raising their innocent hands

Now like a mighty wind they raise to heaven the voice of
    song
Or like harmonious thunderings the seats of Heaven among
Beneath them sit the aged men, wise guardians of the poor
Then cherish pity, lest you drive an angel from your door

# The Chimney Sweeper

When my mother died I was very young,
And my father sold me while yet my tongue,
Could scarcely cry weep weep weep weep.
So your chimneys I sweep, & in soot I sleep.

Theres little Tom Dacre, who cried when his head
That curl'd like a lamb's back, was shav'd, so I said,
Hush Tom never mind it, for when your head's bare,
You know that the soot cannot spoil your white hair.

And so he was quiet, & that very night,
As Tom was a sleeping he had such a sight,
That thousands of sweepers Dick, Joe Ned & Jack
Were all of them lock'd up in coffins of black

And by came an Angel who had a bright key,
And he open'd the coffins & set them all free.
Then down a green plain leaping laughing they run
And wash in a river and shine in the Sun.

Then naked & white, all their bags left behind,
They rise upon clouds, and sport in the wind.
And the Angel told Tom if he'd be a good boy,
He'd have God for his father & never want joy.

And so Tom awoke and we rose in the dark
And got with our bags & our brushes to work.
Though the morning was cold, Tom was happy & warm,
So if all do their duty, they need not fear harm.

# Infant Sorrow

My mother groand! my father wept.
Into the dangerous world I leapt:
Helpless, naked, piping loud;
Like a fiend hid in a cloud.

Struggling in my fathers hands:
Striving against my swadling bands:
Bound and weary I thought best
To sulk upon my mothers breast.

JOANNA BAILLIE (1762–1851)

# A Mother to Her Waking Infant

Now in thy dazzling half-oped eye,
Thy curlèd nose and lip awry,
Thy up-hoist arms and noddling head,
And little chin with crystal spread,
Poor helpless thing! what do I see,
   That I should sing of thee?

From thy poor tongue no accents come,
Which can but rub thy toothless gum;
Small understanding boasts thy face.
Thy shapeless limbs nor step nor grace;
A few short words thy feats may tell.
   And yet I love thee well.

When sudden wakes the bitter shriek,
And redder swells thy little cheek;
When rattled keys thy woes beguile,
And through the wet eye gleams the smile,
Still for thy weakly self is spent
   Thy little silly plaint.

But when thy friends are in distress,
Thou'lt laugh and chuckle ne'er the less;
Nor e'en with sympathy be smitten,
Though all are sad but thee and kitten;
Yet little varlet that thou art,
   Thou twitchest at the heart.

Thy rosy cheek so soft and warm;
Thy pinky hand and dimpled arm;
Thy silken locks that scantly peep,

With gold-tipped ends, where circles deep
Around thy neck in harmless grace
So soft and sleekly hold their place,
Might harder hearts with kindness fill,
 And gain our right good will.

Each passing clown bestows his blessing,
Thy mouth is worn with old wives' kissing:
E'en lighter looks the gloomy eye
Of surly sense, when thou art by;
And yet I think whoe'er they be,
 They love thee not like me.

Perhaps when time shall add a few
Short years to thee, thou'lt love me too.
Then wilt thou through life's weary way
Become my sure and cheering stay:
Wilt care for me, and be my hold,
 When I am weak and old.

Thou'lt listen to my lengthened tale,
And pity me when I am frail –
But see, the sweepy spinning fly
Upon the window takes thine eye,
Go to thy little senseless play –
 Thou dost not heed my lay.

# from *The Prelude*: Book First
### (Childhood and School-Time)

Oh! many a time have I, a five years' Child,
A naked Boy, in one delightful Rill,
A little Mill-race severed from his stream,
Made one long bathing of a summer's day,
Basked in the sun, and plunged, and basked again
Alternate all a summer's day, or coursed
Over the sandy fields, leaping through groves
Of yellow grunsel, or when crag and hill,
The woods, and distant Skiddaw's lofty height,
Were bronzed with a deep radiance, stood alone
Beneath the sky, as if I had been born
On Indian Plains, and from my Mother's hut
Had run abroad in wantonness, to sport,
A naked Savage, in the thunder shower.

Fair seed-time had my soul, and I grew up
Fostered alike by beauty and by fear;
Much favoured in my birthplace, and no less
In that beloved Vale to which, erelong,
I was transplanted. Well I call to mind
('Twas at an early age, ere I had seen
Nine summers) when upon the mountain slope
The frost and breath of frosty wind had snapped
The last autumnal crocus, 'twas my joy
To wander half the night among the Cliffs
And the smooth Hollows, where the woodcocks ran
Along the open turf. In thought and wish
That time, my shoulder all with springes hung,
I was a fell destroyer. On the heights

Scudding away from snare to snare, I plied
My anxious visitation, hurrying on,
Still hurrying, hurrying onward; moon and stars
Were shining o'er my head; I was alone,
And seemed to be a trouble to the peace
That was among them. Sometimes it befel
In these night-wanderings, that a strong desire
O'erpowered my better reason, and the bird
Which was the captive of another's toils
Became my prey; and, when the deed was done
I heard among the solitary hills
Low breathings coming after me, and sounds
Of undistinguishable motion, steps
Almost as silent as the turf they trod.

Nor less in springtime when on southern banks
The shining sun had from his knot of leaves
Decoyed the primrose flower, and when the Vales
And woods were warm, was I a plunderer then
In the high places, on the lonesome peaks
Where'er, among the mountains and the winds,
The Mother Bird had built her lodge. Though mean
My object, and inglorious, yet the end
Was not ignoble. Oh! when I have hung
Above the raven's nest, by knots of grass
And half-inch fissures in the slippery rock
But ill sustained, and almost, as it seemed,
Suspended by the blast which blew amain,
Shouldering the naked crag; Oh! at that time,
While on the perilous ridge I hung alone,
With what strange utterance did the loud dry wind
Blow through my ears! the sky seemed not a sky
Of earth, and with what motion moved the clouds!

[41]

The mind of Man is framed even like the breath
And harmony of music. There is a dark
Invisible workmanship that reconciles
Discordant elements, and makes them move
In one society. Ah me! that all
The terrors, all the early miseries
Regrets, vexations, lassitudes, that all
The thoughts and feelings which have been infused
Into my mind, should ever have made up
The calm existence that is mine when I
Am worthy of myself! Praise to the end!
Thanks likewise for the means! But I believe
That Nature, oftentimes, when she would frame
A favored Being, from his earliest dawn
Of infancy doth open out the clouds,
As at the touch of lightning, seeking him
With gentlest visitation; not the less,
Though haply aiming at the self-same end,
Does it delight her sometimes to employ
Severer interventions, ministry
More palpable, and so she dealt with me.

One evening (surely I was led by her)
I went alone into a Shepherd's Boat,
A Skiff that to a Willow tree was tied
Within a rocky Cave, its usual home.
'Twas by the shores of Patterdale, a Vale
Wherein I was a Stranger, thither come
A School-boy Traveller, at the Holidays.
Forth rambled from the Village Inn alone
No sooner had I sight of this small Skiff,
Discovered thus by unexpected chance,
Than I unloosed her tether and embarked.

The moon was up, the Lake was shining clear
Among the hoary mountains; from the Shore
I pushed, and struck the oars and struck again
In cadence, and my little Boat moved on
Even like a Man who walks with stately step
Though bent on speed. It was an act of stealth
And troubled pleasure; not without the voice
Of mountain-echoes did my Boat move on,
Leaving behind her still on either side
Small circles glittering idly in the moon,
Until they melted all into one track
Of sparkling light. A rocky Steep uprose
Above the Cavern of the Willow tree
And now, as suited one who proudly rowed
With his best skill, I fixed a steady view
Upon the top of that same craggy ridge,
The bound of the horizon, for behind
Was nothing but the stars and the grey sky.
She was an elfin Pinnace; lustily
I dipped my oars into the silent Lake,
And, as I rose upon the stroke, my Boat
Went heaving through the water, like a Swan;
When from behind that craggy Steep, till then
The bound of the horizon, a huge Cliff,
As if with voluntary power instinct,
Upreared its head. I struck, and struck again
And, growing still in stature, the huge Cliff
Rose up between me and the stars, and still,
With measured motion, like a living thing,
Strode after me. With trembling hands I turned,
And through the silent water stole my way
Back to the Cavern of the Willow tree.
There, in her mooring-place, I left my Bark,

And, through the meadows homeward went, with grave
And serious thoughts; and after I had seen
That spectacle, for many days, my brain
Worked with a dim and undetermined sense
Of unknown modes of being; in my thoughts
There was a darkness, call it solitude,
Or blank desertion, no familiar shapes
Of hourly objects, images of trees,
Of sea or sky, no colours of green fields;
But huge and mighty Forms that do not live
Like living men moved slowly through the mind
By day and were the trouble of my dreams.

# Ode: Intimations of Immortality from Recollections of Early Childhood

*The child is father of the man;*
*And I could wish my days to be*
*Bound each to each by natural piety.*
(– 'My heart leaps up when I behold')

I

There was a time when meadow, grove, and stream,
The earth, and every common sight,
        To me did seem
        Apparelled in celestial light,
The glory and the freshness of a dream.
It is not now as it hath been of yore; –
        Turn wheresoe'er I may,
        By night or day.
The things which I have seen I now can see no more.

II

        The Rainbow comes and goes,
        And lovely is the Rose,
        The Moon doth with delight
Look round her when the heavens are bare,
        Waters on a starry night
        Are beautiful and fair;
    The sunshine is a glorious birth;
    But yet I know, where'er I go,
That there hath past away a glory from the earth.

III

Now, while the birds thus sing a joyous song,
    And while the young lambs bound
        As to the tabor's sound,

To me alone there came a thought of grief:
A timely utterance gave that thought relief,
  And I again am strong:
The cataracts blow their trumpets from the steep;
No more shall grief of mine the season wrong;
I hear the Echoes through the mountains throng,
The Winds come to me from the fields of sleep,
   And all the earth is gay;
    Land and sea
  Give themselves up to jollity,
   And with the heart of May
  Doth every Beast keep holiday; –
   Thou Child of Joy,
Shout round me, let me hear thy shouts, thou happy
 Shepherd-boy!

 IV
Ye blessèd Creatures, I have heard the call
 Ye to each other make; I see
The heavens laugh with you in your jubilee;
 My heart is at your festival,
  My head hath its coronal,
The fulness of your bliss, I feel – I feel it all.
  Oh evil day! if I were sullen
  While Earth herself is adorning,
   This sweet May-morning,
  And the Children are culling
   On every side,
  In a thousand valleys far and wide,
  Fresh flowers; while the sun shines warm,
And the Babe leaps up on his Mother's arm: –
  I hear, I hear, with joy I hear!
  – But there's a Tree, of many, one,

A single field which I have looked upon,
Both of them speak of something that is gone;
    The Pansy at my feet
    Doth the same tale repeat:
Whither is fled the visionary gleam?
Where is it now, the glory and the dream?

    V

Our birth is but a sleep and a forgetting:
The Soul that rises with us, our life's Star,
    Hath had elsewhere its setting,
      And cometh from afar:
    Not in entire forgetfulness,
    And not in utter nakedness,
But trailing clouds of glory do we come
    From God, who is our home:
Heaven lies about us in our infancy!
Shades of the prison-house begin to close
    Upon the growing Boy,
      But He
Beholds the light, and whence it flows,
    He sees it in his joy;
The Youth, who daily farther from the east
    Must travel, still is Nature's Priest,
    And by the vision splendid
    Is on his way attended;
At length the Man perceives it die away,
And fade into the light of common day.

    VI

Earth fills her lap with pleasures of her own;
Yearnings she hath in her own natural kind,
And, even with something of a Mother's mind,
    And no unworthy aim,

The homely Nurse doth all she can
To make her Foster-child, her Inmate Man,
    Forget the glories he hath known,
And that imperial palace whence he came.

VII

Behold the Child among his new-born blisses,
A six years' Darling of a pigmy size!
See, where 'mid work of his own hand he lies,
Fretted by sallies of his mother's kisses,
With light upon him from his father's eyes!
See, at his feet, some little plan or chart,
Some fragment from his dream of human life,
Shaped by himself with newly-learnèd art
    A wedding or a festival,
    A mourning or a funeral;
      And this hath now his heart,
    And unto this he frames his song:
      Then will he fit his tongue
To dialogues of business, love, or strife;
    But it will not be long
    Ere this be thrown aside,
    And with new joy and pride
The little Actor cons another part;
Filling from time to time his 'humorous stage'
With all the Persons, down to palsied Age,
That Life brings with her in her equipage;
    As if his whole vocation
    Were endless imitation.

VIII

Thou, whose exterior semblance doth belie
    Thy Soul's immensity;
Thou best Philosopher, who yet dost keep

Thy heritage, thou Eye among the blind,
That, deaf and silent, read'st the eternal deep,
Haunted for ever by the eternal mind, —
　　　Mighty Prophet! Seer blest!
　　　On whom those truths do rest,
Which we are toiling all our lives to find,
In darkness lost, the darkness of the grave;
Thou, over whom thy Immortality
Broods like the Day, a Master o'er a Slave,
A Presence which is not to be put by;
Thou little Child, yet glorious in the might
Of heaven-born freedom on thy being's height,
Why with such earnest pains dost thou provoke
The years to bring the inevitable yoke,
Thus blindly with thy blessedness at strife?
Full soon thy Soul shall have her earthly freight,
And custom lie upon thee with a weight,
Heavy as frost, and deep almost as life!

　IX
　　　O joy! that in our embers
　　　Is something that doth live,
　　　That Nature yet remembers
　　　What was so fugitive!
The thought of our past years in me doth breed
Perpetual benediction: not indeed
For that which is most worthy to be blest;
Delight and liberty, the simple creed
Of Childhood, whether busy or at rest,
With new–fledged hope still fluttering in his breast: —
　　　Not for these I raise
　　　The song of thanks and praise
　　But for those obstinate questionings

Of sense and outward things,
Fallings from us, vanishings;
Blank misgivings of a Creature
Moving about in worlds not realised,
High instincts before which our mortal Nature
Did tremble like a guilty thing surprised:
But for those first affections,
Those shadowy recollections,
Which, be they what they may
Are yet the fountain-light of all our day,
Are yet a master-light of all our seeing;
Uphold us, cherish, and have power to make
Our noisy years seem moments in the being
Of the eternal Silence: truths that wake,
To perish never;
Which neither listlessness, nor mad endeavour,
Nor Man nor Boy,
Nor all that is at enmity with joy,
Can utterly abolish or destroy!
Hence in a season of calm weather
Though inland far we be,
Our Souls have sight of that immortal sea
Which brought us hither,
Can in a moment travel thither,
And see the Children sport upon the shore,
And hear the mighty waters rolling evermore.

x

Then sing, ye Birds, sing, sing a joyous song!
And let the young Lambs bound
As to the tabor's sound!
We in thought will join your throng,
Ye that pipe and ye that play,

Ye that through your hearts to-day
Feel the gladness of the May!
What though the radiance which was once so bright
Be now for ever taken from my sight,
Though nothing can bring back the hour
Of splendour in the grass, of glory in the flower;
We will grieve not, rather find
Strength in what remains behind;
In the primal sympathy
Which having been must ever be;
In the soothing thoughts that spring
Out of human suffering;
In the faith that looks through death,
In years that bring the philosophic mind.

XI

And O, ye Fountains, Meadows, Hills, and Groves,
Forebode not any severing of our loves!
Yet in my heart of hearts I feel your might;
I only have relinquished one delight
To live beneath your more habitual sway.
I love the Brooks which down their channels fret,
Even more than when I tripped lightly as they;
The innocent brightness of a new–born Day
Is lovely yet;
The Clouds that gather round the setting sun
Do take a sober colouring from an eye
That hath kept watch o'er man's mortality;
Another race hath been, and other palms are won.
Thanks to the human heart by which we live,
Thanks to its tenderness, its joys, and fears,
To me the meanest flower that blows can give
Thoughts that do often lie too deep for tears.

SAMUEL TAYLOR COLERIDGE (1772–1834)

# Frost at Midnight

The Frost performs its secret ministry,
Unhelp'd by any wind. The owlet's cry
Came loud – and hark, again! loud as before.
The inmates of my cottage, all at rest,
Have left me to that solitude, which suits
Abstruser musings: save that at my side
My cradled infant slumbers peacefully.
'Tis calm indeed! so calm, that it disturbs
And vexes meditation with its strange
And extreme silentness. Sea, hill, and wood,
This populous village! Sea, and hill, and wood,
With all the numberless goings-on of life,
Inaudible as dreams! the thin blue flame
Lies on my low-burnt fire, and quivers not;
Only that film, which fluttered on the grate,
Still flutters there, the sole unquiet thing.
Methinks, its motion in this hush of nature
Gives it dim sympathies with me who live,
Making it a companionable form,
Whose puny flaps and freaks the idling Spirit
By its own moods interprets, every where
Echo or mirror seeking of itself,
And makes a toy of Thought.

                                    But O! how oft,
How oft, at school, with most believing mind,
Presageful, have I gazed upon the bars,
To watch that fluttering *stranger*! and as oft
With unclosed lids, already had I dreamt
Of my sweet birth-place, and the old church-tower,

Whose bells, the poor man's only music, rang
From morn to evening, all the hot Fair-day,
So sweetly, that they stirred and haunted me
With a wild pleasure, falling on mine ear
Most like articulate sounds of things to come!
So gazed I, till the soothing things, I dreamt,
Lulled me to sleep, and sleep prolonged my dreams!
And so I brooded all the following morn,
Awed by the stern preceptor's face, mine eye
Fixed with mock study on my swimming book:
Save if the door half opened, and I snatched
A hasty glance, and still my heart leaped up,
For still I hoped to see the stranger's face,
Townsman, or aunt, or sister more beloved,
My play-mate when we both were clothed alike!

Dear Babe, that sleepest cradled by my side,
Whose gentle breathings, heard in this deep calm,
Fill up the interspersed vacancies
And momentary pauses of the thought!
My babe so beautiful! it thrills my heart
With tender gladness, thus to look at thee,
And think that thou shall learn far other lore,
And in far other scenes! For I was reared
In the great city, pent 'mid cloisters dim,
And saw nought lovely but the sky and stars.
But *thou*, my babe! shalt wander like a breeze
By lakes and sandy shores, beneath the crags
Of ancient mountain, and beneath the clouds,
Which image in their bulk both lakes and shores
And mountain crags: so shalt thou see and hear
The lovely shapes and sounds intelligible
Of that eternal language, which thy God

Utters, who from eternity doth teach
Himself in all, and all things in himself.
Great universal Teacher! he shall mould
Thy spirit, and by giving make it ask.

Therefore all seasons shall be sweet to thee,
Whether the summer clothe the general earth
With greenness, or the redbreast sit and sing
Betwixt the tufts of snow on the bare branch
Of mossy apple-tree, while the nigh thatch
Smokes in the sun-thaw; whether the eave-drops fall
Heard only in the trances of the blast,
Or if the secret ministry of frost
Shall hang them up in silent icicles,
Quietly shining to the quiet Moon.

BERNARD BARTON (1784–1849)

## Haunts of Childhood

*'O long be my heart with such memories fill'd!*
*Like the vase in which roses have once been distill'd;*
*You may break, you may ruin the vase if you will,*
*But the scent of the roses will hang round it still.'*
— Moore

Who has not known and felt the soothing charm
Of looking back to hours, so clear and calm,
They seem as if they scarce were spent on earth,
But ow'd to mere imagination birth?
He most enjoys them, who in childhood slighted
Their present bliss; – whose eager eye delighted
The shadowy joys of future years to scan,
And sigh'd, most foolishly, to be a man!

We need not sleep to dream. – I was not sleeping;
But busy memory was her vigils keeping;
And on my mind past images were thronging,
Bringing those feelings to the past belonging;
They came so thick about me, that at last,
I fairly lost the present in the past;
And, for a time, a happy boy again,
I lost in memory's pleasure, manhood's pain.
I stroll'd along a winding lane: a stream
Flow'd on one side of it; the sun's bright beam
Was here and there reflected, gaily glancing,
As o'er its pebbly bed that brook was dancing:
Sometimes, so narrow were its banks, the eye
Could scarcely trace it in its revelry;
Half hid by stunted bushes, on it flow'd;
Now still, now murmuring sweetly on its road: –
A wooden bridge then cross'd it, and I stood

[ 55 ]

Awhile upon that bridge in pensive mood,
To look around me.

                 Straight before me rose
A house, where all was hush'd in calm repose;
For 'twas a summer morning, bright and fair,
And none of human kind were near me there:
Before the house there were some lofty trees,
Whose topmost branches felt the morning breeze,
And glisten'd in the sunbeams; these among
Were numerous rooks, attending on their young,
Whose clamorous cawings, as they hover'd round,
Seem'd to my ear like Music's sweetest sound.
Below, before the house, there was a space,
Where in two rows were set, with bloomy grace,
Orange and lemon trees; which to the sun
Open'd their fragrant blossoms every one;
And round them bees all busily were humming,
Cheerily to their morning labours coming: –
And in the centre of each space beside,
An aloe spread its prickly leaves with pride.

Now in the garden of that house I stray'd,
Its flowers, its mossy turf, its walks survey'd;
Explor'd each nook, and roam'd through each recess,
With pleasure, and light-hearted carelessness:
Nor was it long before I found a walk
Where I could think, or to myself could talk; –
A grassy walk, with lime trees on one side,
Bordering a pond which yet they did not hide;
For here and there upon its rippling bosom
The water lily op'd her dewy blossom;
And at the end of this sweet walk I found
A grotto, where I listen'd to the sound

Of turtle-doves, which in a room above,
Were tremulously telling tales of love.

But wherefore dwell upon these recollections,
These hallow'd haunts of childhood's warm affections?
Why? but because they rise with wings of healing,
And hover round me; softly, sweetly stealing
Its bitterest pang from pain, its sting from sorrow,
And from past blessedness fresh blessings borrow.
O! ere such dreams as these for ever leave me,
Or manhood of such blameless bliss bereave me;
Memory, and life itself, must both be past,
For while I live, at times, must their remembrance last.

GEORGE GORDON, LORD BYRON (1788–1824)

# On A Distant View of the Village and School of Harrow on the Hill, 1806

*Oh! mihi præteritos referat si Jupiter annos.* – Virgil

Ye scenes of my childhood, whose lov'd recollection
    Embitters the present, compar'd with the past;
Where science first dawn'd on the powers of reflection,
    And friendships were form'd, too romantic to last;

Where fancy, yet, joys to retrace the resemblance
    Of comrades, in friendship and mischief allied;
How welcome to me your ne'er fading remembrance,
    Which rests in the bosom, though hope is deny'd!

Again I revisit the hills where we sported,
    The streams where we swam, and the fields where we
        fought;
The school where, loud warn'd by the bell, we resorted,
    To pore o'er the precepts by Pedagogues taught.

Again I behold where for hours I have ponder'd,
    As reclining, at eve, on yon tombstone I lay;
Or round the steep brow of the churchyard I wander'd,
    To catch the last gleam of the sun's setting ray.

I once more view the room, with spectators surrounded,
    Where, as Zanga, I trod on Alonzo o'erthrown;
While, to swell my young pride, such applauses resounded,
    I fancied that Mossop himself was outshone.

Or, as Lear, I pour'd forth the deep imprecation,
    By my daughters, of kingdom and reason depriv'd;
Till, fir'd by loud plaudits and self-adulation,
    I regarded myself as a *Garrick* reviv'd.

Ye dreams of my boyhood, how much I regret you!
  Unfaded your memory dwells in my breast;
Though sad and deserted, I ne'er can forget you:
  Your pleasures may still be in fancy possest.

To Ida full oft may remembrance restore me,
  While Fate shall the shades of the future unroll!
Since Darkness o'ershadows the prospect before me,
  More dear is the beam of the past to my soul!

But if, through the course of the years which await me,
  Some new scene of pleasure should open to view,
I will say, while with rapture the thought shall elate me,
  Oh! such were the days which my infancy knew.

PERCY BYSSHE SHELLEY (1792–1822)

# To William Shelley

### I

The billows on the beach are leaping around it,
 The bark is weak and frail,
The sea looks black, and the clouds that bound it
 Darkly strew the gale.
Come with me, thou delightful child,
Come with me, though the wave is wild,
And the winds are loose, we must not stay,
Or the slaves of the law may rend thee away.

### II

They have taken thy brother and sister dear,
 They have made them unfit for thee;
They have withered the smile and dried the tear
 Which should have been sacred to me.
To a blighting faith and a cause of crime
They have bound them slaves in youthly prime,
And they will curse my name and thee
Because we fearless are and free.

### III

Come thou, beloved as thou art;
 Another sleepeth still
Near thy sweet mother's anxious heart,
 Which thou with joy shalt fill,
With fairest smiles of wonder thrown
On that which is indeed our own,
And which in distant lands will be
The dearest playmate unto thee.

IV

Fear not the tyrants will rule for ever,
 Or the priests of the evil faith;
They stand on the brink of that raging river,
 Whose waves they have tainted with death.
It is fed from the depths of a thousand dells,
Around them it foams and rages and swells;
And their swords and their sceptres I floating see,
Like wrecks on the surge of eternity.

V

Rest, rest, and shriek not, thou gentle child!
 The rocking of the boat thou fearest,
And the cold spray and the clamour wild? –
 There, sit between us two, thou dearest –
Me and thy mother – well we know
The storm at which thou tremblest so,
With all its dark and hungry graves,
Less cruel than the savage slaves
Who hunt us o'er these sheltering waves.

VI

This hour will in thy memory
 Be a dream of days forgotten long.
We soon shall dwell by the azure sea
Of serene and golden Italy,
Or Greece, the Mother of the free;
 And I will teach thine infant tongue
To call upon those heroes old
In their own language, and will mould
Thy growing spirit in the flame
Of Grecian lore, that by such name
A patriot's birthright thou mayst claim!

JOHN CLARE (1793–1864)

## Sonnet

Childhood meets joys so easy every where
Charmd & delighted wi but every scene
Ah was I still a child the names so dear
How odd a change of feelings intervene
Still former things that pleasd me interfere
& I may view them but its usless now
No joys abound for me – still sad & drear
My eye turns from them like as autumns bough
Is stript of foliage by the winter winds
So the rough usuage manhoods station finds
Sweet childhoods every feeling sweeps away
Choaking the ripling channel whence they flow
Forbidding every flower of bliss to stay
To give the naked stem a keener blow

# On Re-perusing, After a Long Interval, a Book that had been a Favourite in Childhood

Wakener of thoughts in youth's sweet spring of life,
Thou hast brought back that time when all was new,
I glance at once long years of turmoil through,
And rest, where all with peace and flowers is rife.
  How, as this long-forsaken tome I view,
Sinks into deepest shadow manhood's strife;
  And all my childish joys at once renew;
As if each word was magic that I read,
Of power to wake the past, and raise the dead;
  Giving the spirit of lost joys so plain,
  My worn heart beats with youth's bold pulse again.
Oh volume, potent as that book of dread,
  Which, for his Ladye, he of Deloraine,
  From wizard Scott, bore with such toil and pain!

There may be tomes more deep, more rare, more good
  Than thou, companion of my childish days;
But thou'rt the first I lov'd and understood!
  Thou art the first plung'd me in wonder's maze!
I cling to thee, as early lover should;
  Thrill with those feelings thou wert first to raise;
  I stray with thee through all past pleasant ways;
Recall the converse we have had together,
Reclin'd on grassy bank, in summer weather,
  Or by a winter fire, in antique chair;
  And, like a lover gazing on his fair,
I find new beauties out at each fresh gaze.
  Let Wisdom frown; she'd try to yield, in vain,
  Such joy as from thy simple page I gain!

# Childhood

Oh what a wilderness were this sad world
If man were always man, and never child;
If Nature gave no time, so sweetly wild,
When every thought is deftly crisped and curled,
Like fragrant hyacinth with dew impearled,
And every feeling in itself confiding,
Yet never single, but continuous, gliding
With wavy motion as, on wings unfurled,
A seraph clips Empyreal! Such man was
Ere sin had made him know himself too well.
No child was born ere that primeval loss.
What might have been, no living soul can tell:
But Heaven is kind, and therefore all possess
Once in their life fair Eden's simpleness.

THOMAS HOOD (1799–1845)

## 'I Remember, I Remember'

I remember, I remember,
The house where I was born,
The little window where the sun
Came peeping in at morn;
He never came a wink too soon,
Nor brought too long a day,
But now, I often wish the night
Had borne my breath away!

I remember, I remember,
The roses, red and white,
The vi'lets, and the lily-cups,
Those flowers made of light!
The lilacs where the robin built,
And where my brother set
The laburnum on his birthday, –
The tree is living yet!

I remember, I remember,
Where I was used to swing,
And thought the air must rush as fresh
To swallows on the wing;
My spirit flew in feathers then,
That is so heavy now,
The summer pools could hardly cool
The fever on my brow!

I remember, I remember,
The fir-trees dark and high;
I used to think their slender tops
Were close against the sky:

It was a childish ignorance,
But now 'tis little joy
To know I'm farther off from heav'n
Than when I was a boy.

# Childhood

Aye, at that time our days wer but vew,
An' our lim's wer but small, an' a-growèn;
An' then the feäir worold wer new,
An' life wer all hopevul an' gaÿ;
An' the times o' the sproutèn o' leaves,
An' the cheäk-burnèn seasons o' mowèn,
An' bindèn o' red-headed sheaves,
Wer all welcome seasons o' jaÿ.

Then the housen seem'd high, that be low,
An' the brook did seem wide that is narrow,
An' time, that do vlee, did goo slow,
An' veelèns now feeble wer strong,
An' our worold did end wi' the neämes
Ov the Sha'sbury Hill or Bulbarrow;
An' life did seem only the geämes
That we plaÿ'd as the days rolled along.

Then the rivers, an' high-timber'd lands,
An' the zilvery hills, 'ithout buyèn,
Did seem to come into our hands
Vrom others that own'd em avore;
An' all zickness, an' sorrow, an' need,
Seem'd to die wi' the wold vo'k a-dyèn,
An' leäve us vor ever a-freed
Vrom evils our forefathers bore.

But happy be childern the while
They have elders a-livèn to love em,
An' teäke all the wearisome tweil
That zome hands or others mus' do;

[67]

Like the low-headed shrubs that be warm,
In the lewth o' the trees up above em,
A-screen'd vrom the cwold blowèn storm
That the timber avore em must rue.

## The Cry of the Children

'φεῦ, φεῦ, τί προσδέρκεσθέ μ' ὄμμασιν, τέκνα.'
[Alas, alas, why do you gaze at me with your eyes, my children.]
– Medea

Do ye hear the children weeping, O my brothers,
  Ere the sorrow comes with years?
They are leaning their young heads against their mothers, –
  And *that* cannot stop their tears.
The young lambs are bleating in the meadows;
  The young birds are chirping in the nest;
The young fawns are playing with the shadows;
  The young flowers are blowing toward the west –
But the young, young children, O my brothers,
  They are weeping bitterly! –
They are weeping in the playtime of the others,
  In the country of the free.

Do you question the young children in the sorrow,
  Why their tears are falling so? –
The old man may weep for his to-morrow
  Which is lost in Long Ago –
The old tree is leafless in the forest –
  The old year is ending in the frost –
The old wound, if stricken, is the sorest –
  The old hope is hardest to be lost:
But the young, young children, O my brothers,
  Do you ask them why they stand
Weeping sore before the bosoms of their mothers,
  In our happy Fatherland?

They look up with their pale and sunken faces,
  And their looks are sad to see,

For the man's grief abhorrent, draws and presses
     Down the cheeks of infancy –
'Your old earth,' they say, 'is very dreary;'
     'Our young feet,' they say, 'are very weak!
Few paces have we taken, yet are weary –
     Our grave-rest is very far to seek!
Ask the old why they weep, and not the children,
     For the outside earth is cold –
And we young ones stand without, in our bewildering,
     And the graves are for the old!

'True,' say the young children, 'it may happen
     That we die before our time!
Little Alice died last year – the grave is shapen
     Like a snowball, in the rime.
We looked into the pit prepared to take her –
     Was no room for any work in the close clay:
From the sleep wherein she lieth none will wake her,
     Crying, "Get up, little Alice! it is day."
If you listen by that grave, in sun and shower,
     With your ear down, little Alice never cries;
Could we see her face, be sure we should not know her,
     For the smile has time for growing in her eyes, –
And merry go her moments, lulled and stilled in
     The shroud, by the kirk-chime!
It is good when it happens,' say the children,
     'That we die before our time!'

Alas, the wretched children! they are seeking
     Death in life, as best to have!
They are binding up their hearts away from breaking,
     With a cerement from the grave.
Go out, children, from the mine and from the city –
     Sing out, children, as the little thrushes do –

Pluck you handfuls of the meadow-cowslips pretty
    Laugh aloud, to feel your fingers let them through!
But they answer, 'Are your cowslips of the meadows
        Like our weeds anear the mine?
Leave us quiet in the dark of the coal-shadows,
        From your pleasures fair and fine!

'For oh,' say the children, 'we are weary,
        And we cannot run or leap –
If we cared for any meadows, it were merely
        To drop down in them and sleep.
Our knees tremble sorely in the stooping –
    We fall upon our faces, trying to go;
And, underneath our heavy eyelids drooping,
    The reddest flower would look as pale as snow.
For, all day, we drag our burden tiring,
        Through the coal-dark, underground –
Or, all day, we drive the wheels of iron
        In the factories, round and round.

'For all day, the wheels are droning, turning, –
        Their wind comes in our faces, –
Till our hearts turn, – our heads, with pulses burning,
        And the walls turn in their places –
Turns the sky in the high window blank and reeling –
    Turns the long light that droppeth down the wall, –
Turn the black flies that crawl along the ceiling –
    All are turning, all the day, and we with all! –
And all day, the iron wheels are droning;
        And sometimes we could pray,
"O ye wheels," (breaking out in a mad moaning)
        "Stop! be silent for to-day !" '

Ay! be silent! Let them hear each other breathing
        For a moment, mouth to mouth –

[71]

Let them touch each other's hands, in a fresh wreathing
        Of their tender human youth!
Let them feel that this cold metallic motion
    Is not all the life God fashions or reveals –
Let them prove their inward souls against the notion
    That they live in you, or under you, O wheels! –
Still, all day, the iron wheels go onward,
        As if Fate in each were stark;
And the children's souls, which God is calling sunward,
        Spin on blindly in the dark.

Now tell the poor young children, O my brothers,
        To look up to Him and pray –
So the blessed One, who blesseth all the others,
        Will bless them another day.
They answer, 'Who is God that He should hear us,
    While the rushing of the iron wheels is stirred?
When we sob aloud, the human creatures near us
    Pass by, hearing not, or answer not a word!
And we hear not (for the wheels in their resounding)
        Strangers speaking at the door:
Is it likely God, with angels singing round Him,
        Hears our weeping any more?

'Two words, indeed, of praying we remember;
        And at midnight's hour of harm, –
"Our Father," looking upward in the chamber,
        We say softly for a charm.
We know no other words, except "Our Father,"
    And we think that, in some pause of angels' song,
God may pluck them with the silence sweet to gather,
    And hold both within His right hand which is strong.
"Our Father!" If He heard us, He would surely
        (For they call Him good and mild)

[ 72 ]

Answer, smiling down the steep world very purely,
  "Come and rest with me, my child." '

'But, no!' say the children, weeping faster,
  'He is speechless as a stone;
And they tell us, of His image is the master
  Who commands us to work on.
Go to!' say the children, – 'Up in Heaven,
  Dark, wheel-like, turning clouds are all we find!
Do not mock us; grief has made us unbelieving –
  We look up for God, but tears have made us blind.'
Do ye hear the children weeping and disproving,
  O my brothers, what ye preach?
For God's possible is taught by His world's loving –
  And the children doubt of each.

And well may the children weep before you;
  They are weary ere they run;
They have never seen the sunshine, nor the glory
  Which is brighter than the sun:
They know the grief of man, without its wisdom;
  They sink in the despair, without its calm –
Are slaves, without the liberty in Christdom, –
  Are martyrs, by the pang without the palm, –
Are worn, as if with age, yet unretrievingly
  No dear remembrance keep, –
Are orphans of the earthly love and heavenly:
  Let them weep! let them weep!

They look up, with their pale and sunken faces,
  And their look is dread to see,
For they think you see their angels in their places,
  With eyes meant for Deity; –
'How long,' they say, 'how long, O cruel nation,

Will you stand, to move the world, on a child's heart, –
Stifle down with a mailed heel its palpitation,
    And tread onward to your throne amid the mart?
Our blood splashes upward, O our tyrants,
        And your purple shews your path;
But the child's sob curseth deeper in the silence
        Than the strong man in his wrath!'

## from *In Memoriam A.H.H.*
### OBIIT MDCCCXXXIII

[XLV]

The baby new to earth and sky,
    What time his tender palm is prest
    Against the circle of the breast,
Has never thought that 'this is I:'

But as he grows he gathers much,
    And learns the use of 'I,' and 'me,'
    And finds 'I am not what I see,
And other than the things I touch.'

So rounds he to a separate mind
    From whence clear memory may begin,
    As thro' the frame that binds him in
His isolation grows defined.

This use may lie in blood and breath,
    Which else were fruitless of their due,
    Had man to learn himself anew
Beyond the second birth of Death.

## Rhyme for a Child Viewing a Naked Venus in a Painting of 'the Judgement of Paris'

He gazed and gazed and gazed and gazed,
Amazed, amazed, amazed, amazed.

EMILY BRONTË (1818–48)

## 'Tell me tell me Smiling Child'

Tell me tell me smiling child
What the past is like to thee?
An Autumn evening soft and mild
With a wind that sighs mournfully

Tell me what is the present hour?
A green and flowery spray
Where a young bird sits gathering its power
To mount and fly away

And what is the future happy one?
A sea beneath a cloudless sun
A mighty, glorious, dazzling sea
Stretching into infinity

# There was a Child went Forth

There was a child went forth every day,
And the first object he look'd upon, that object he became,
And that object became part of him for the day or a certain
    part of the day, or for many years or stretching cycles of
    years.

The early lilacs became part of this child,
And grass and white and red morning-glories, and white
    and red clover, and the song of the phoebe-bird,
And the Third-month lambs and the sow's pink-faint litter,
    and the mare's foal and the cow's calf,
And the noisy brood of the barnyard or by the mire of the
    pond-side,
And the fish suspending themselves so curiously below
    there – and the beautiful curious liquid,
And the water-plants with their graceful flat heads – all
    became part of him.

The field-sprouts of Fourth-month and Fifth-month became
    part of him,
Winter-grain sprouts and those of the light-yellow corn,
    and the esculent roots of the garden,
And the apple-trees cover'd with blossoms and the fruit
    afterward, and wood-berries, and the commonest weeds
    by the road,
And the old drunkard staggering home from the outhouse
    of the tavern whence he had lately risen,
And the school-mistress that pass'd on her way to the school,
And the friendly boys that pass'd – and the quarrelsome
    boys,

And the tidy and fresh-cheek'd girls – and the barefoot
   negro boy and girl,
And all the changes of city and country wherever he went.

His own parents, he that had father'd him and she that had
   conceiv'd him in her womb and birth'd him,
They gave this child more of themselves than that,
They gave him afterward every day – they became part of
   him.

The mother at home quietly placing the dishes on the
   supper-table,
The mother with mild words – clean her cap and gown, a
   wholesome odour falling off her person and clothes as she
   walks by,
The father, strong, self-sufficient, manly, mean, anger'd,
   unjust,
The blow, the quick loud word, the tight bargain, the crafty
   lure,
The family usages, the language, the company, the
   furniture – the yearning and swelling heart,
Affection that will not be gainsay'd – the sense of what is
   real – the thought if after all it should prove unreal,
The doubts of day-time and the doubts of night-time – the
   curious whether and how,
Whether that which appears so is so, or is it all flashes and
   specks?
Men and women crowding fast in the streets – if they are
   not flashes and specks what are they?
The streets themselves and the facades of houses, and goods
   in the windows,
Vehicles, teams, the heavy-plank'd wharves – the huge
   crossing at the ferries,

The village on the highland seen from afar at sunset, the
    river between,
Shadows, aureola and mist, the light falling on roofs and
    gables of white or brown two miles off,
The schooner near by sleepily dropping down the tide, the
    little boat slack-tow'd astern,
The hurrying tumbling waves, quick-broken crests,
    slapping,
The strata of colour'd clouds, the long bar of maroon-tint
    away solitary by itself – the spread of purity it lies
    motionless in,
The horizon's edge, the flying sea-crow, the fragrance of salt
    marsh and shore mud,
These became part of that child who went forth every day,
    and who now goes, and will always go forth every day.

## *from* Brother and Sister

[VI]

Our brown canal was endless to my thought;
And on its banks I sat in dreamy peace,
Unknowing how the good I loved was wrought,
Untroubled by the fear that it would cease.

Slowly the barges floated into view
Rounding a grassy hill to me sublime
With some Unknown beyond it, whither flew
The parting cuckoo toward a fresh spring time.

The wide-arched bridge, the scented elder-flowers,
The wondrous watery rings that died too soon,
The echoes of the quarry, the still hours
With white robe sweeping-on the shadeless noon,

Were but my growing self, are part of me,
My present Past, my root of piety.

# The Toys

My little son, who looked from thoughtful eyes
And moved and spoke in quiet grown-up wise,
Having my law the seventh time disobeyed,
I struck him, and dismissed
With hard words and unkissed,
His mother, who was patient, being dead.
Then, fearing lest his grief should hinder sleep,
I visited his bed,
But found him slumbering deep,
With darkened eyelids, and their lashes yet
From his late sobbing wet.
And I, with moan,
Kissing away his tears, left others of my own;
For, on a table drawn beside his head,
He had put, within his reach,
A box of counters and a red-veined stone,
A piece of glass abraded by the beach
And six or seven shells,
A bottle with bluebells
And two French copper coins, ranged there with careful art,
To comfort his sad heart.
So when that night I prayed
To God, I wept, and said:
Ah, when at last we lie with tranced breath,
Not vexing Thee in death,
And Thou rememberest of what toys
We made our joys,
How weakly understood,
Thy great commanded good,

Then, fatherly not less
Than I whom Thou hast moulded from the clay,
Thou'lt leave Thy wrath, and say,
'I will be sorry for their childishness.'

WILLIAM ALLINGHAM (1824–89)

## 'The Pure Bright World of Childhood Round us Lies'

The pure bright world of childhood round us lies;
We look thereon with weary clouded eyes.

EMILY DICKINSON (1830–1886)

## 'From all the Jails the Boys and Girls'

From all the Jails the Boys and Girls
Ecstatically leap –
Beloved only Afternoon
That Prison doesn't keep

They storm the Earth and stun the Air,
A Mob of solid Bliss –
Alas – that Frowns should lie in wait
For such a Foe as this –

# 'The Child's Faith is New'

The Child's faith is new –
Whole – like His Principle –
Wide – like the Sunrise
On fresh Eyes –
Never had a Doubt –
Laughs – at a Scruple –
Believes all sham
But Paradise –

Credits the World –
Deems His Dominion
Broadest of Sovereignties –
And Caesar – mean –
In the Comparison –
Baseless Emperor –
Ruler of Nought –
Yet swaying all –

Grown bye and bye
To hold mistaken
His pretty estimates
Of Prickly Things
He gains the skill
Sorrowful – as certain –
Men – to anticipate
Instead of Kings –

## Spring and Fall

*to a young child*

Margaret, are you gríeving
Over Goldengrove unleaving?
Leaves, líke the things of man, you
With your fresh thoughts care for, can you?
Áh! ás the heart grows older
It will come to such sights colder
By and by, nor spare a sigh
Though worlds of wanwood leafmeal lie;
And yet you wíll weep and know why
Now no matter, child, the name:
Sórrow's spríngs áre the same.
Nor mouth had, no nor mind, expressed
What heart heard of, ghost guessed:
It ís the blight man was born for,
It is Margaret you mourn for.

ALICE MEYNELL (1847–1922)

# The Sunderland Children

*On the 183 Sunderland children who lost their lives in a panic
at the Victoria Hall, 16th June, 1883*

This was the surplus childhood, held as cheap!
    Not worth the care which shields
The lambs that are to stay, the corn to reap –
    The promise of the fields.

The nation guards her future. Fruits and grass
    And vegetable life
Are fostered league by league. But oh, the mass
    Of childhood over-rife!

O mass, O units! Oh, the separate story
    Planned for each breather of breath!
This futile young mankind, and transitory,
    Is left to stray to Death.

O promise, presage, menace! Upon these
    A certain seal is laid.
Unkept, unbroken, are the auguries
    These little children made.

For threat is bound with promise; and the nation
    Holds festival of regret
Over these dead – dead in their isolation –
    Wisely. She feared their threat.

ROBERT LOUIS STEVENSON (1850–94)

## To Any Reader

As from the house your mother sees
You playing round the garden trees,
So you may see, if you will look
Through the windows of this book,
Another child, far, far away,
And in another garden, play.
But do not think you can at all,
By knocking on the window, call
That child to hear you. He intent
Is all on his play-business bent.
He does not hear; he will not look,
Nor yet be lured out of this book.
For, long ago, the truth to say,
He has grown up and gone away,
And it is but a child of air
That lingers in the garden there.

# Seven-Year-Old Poets

The Mother closed the copybook, and went away
Content, and very proud, and never saw
In the blue eyes, beneath the pimply forehead,
The horror and loathing in her child's soul.

All day he sweat obedience; was very
Bright; still, some black tics, some traits he had
Seemed to foreshadow sour hypocrisies.
In the dark halls, their mildewed paper peeling,
He passed, stuck out his tongue, then pressed two fists
In his crotch, and shut his eyes to see spots.

A door opened: in the evening lamplight
There he was, gasping on the banisters
In a well of light that hung beneath the roof.
Summer especially, stupid, slow, he always tried
To shut himself up in the cool latrine,
There he could think, be calm, and sniff the air.

Washed from the smells of day, the garden, in winter,
Out behind the house, filled with moonlight;
Stretched below a wall, and rolled in dirt,
Squeezing his dazzled eyes to make visions come,
He only heard the scruffy fruit trees grow.
A pity! The friends he had were puny kids,
The ones with runny eyes that streaked their cheeks,
Who hid thin yellow fingers, smeared with mud,
Beneath old cast-off clothes that stank of shit;
They used to talk like gentle idiots.
If she surprised him in these filthy friendships
His mother grew afraid; the child's deep tenderness

Took her astonishment to task. How good . . .
Her wide blue eyes – but they lie.

Seven years old; he made up novels: life
In the desert, Liberty in transports gleaming,
Forests, suns, shores, swamps! Inspiration
In picture magazines: he looked, red-faced,
At Spanish and Italian girls who laughed.
And when, with brown eyes, wild, in calico,
– She was eight – the workers' girl next door
Played rough, jumped right on top of him
In a corner, onto his back, and pulled his hair,
And he was under her, he bit her ass
Because she wore no panties underneath;
Then, beaten by her, hit with fists and heels,
He took the smell of her skin back to his room.

He hated pale December Sunday afternoons:
With plastered hair, on a mahogany couch,
He read the cabbage-coloured pages of a Bible;
Dreams oppressed him every night in bed.

He hated God, but loved the men he saw
Returning home in dirty working clothes
Through the wild evening air to the edge of town,
Where criers, rolling drums before the edicts,
Made the crowds around them groan and laugh.
– He dreamed of prairies of love, where shining herds,
Perfumes of life, pubescent stalks of gold
Swirled slowly round, and then rose up and flew.

The darkest things in life could move him most;
When in that empty room, the shutters closed,
High and blue, with its bitter humid smell,

He read his novel – always on his mind –
Full of heavy ochre skies and drowning forests,

Flowers of flesh in starry woods uncurled,
Catastrophe, vertigo, pity and disaster!
– While the noises of the neighbourhood swelled
Below – stretched out alone on unbleached
Canvas sheets, a turbulent vision of sails!

ARTHUR CHRISTOPHER BENSON (1862–1925)

# Childhood

What do I remember of the bygone days?
Little of the sorrow, something of the praise.

Pleasant games of childhood, in the pleasant shade,
Toiling at a pleasure, playing at a trade!

Often very weary, never glad to rest,
Taking love and laughter with a reckless zest.

Claiming, howso heedless, still to be approved;
Cold to those that loved me, wroth with those I
 loved.

Now that I am older, what is left behind?
Still the restless wonder, still the childish mind.

Still I take, unthankful, service, love, delight.
Laugh to see the morning, murmur at the night.

Do I doubt Thy goodness, question of Thy will?
Father, Lord, forgive us – we are children still.

# To a Child Dancing in The Wind

### I

Dance there upon the shore;
What need have you to care
For wind or water's roar?
And tumble out your hair
That the salt drops have wet;
Being young you have not known
The fool's triumph, nor yet
Love lost as soon as won,
Nor the best labourer dead
And all the sheaves to bind.
What need have you to dread
The monstrous crying of wind?

### II

Has no one said those daring
Kind eyes should be more learn'd?
Or warned you how despairing
The moths are when they are burned?
I could have warned you, but you are young,
So we speak a different tongue.

O you will take whatever's offered
And dream that all the world's a friend,
Suffer as your mother suffered,
Be as broken in the end.
But I am old and you are young,
And I speak a barbarous tongue.

LAURENCE BINYON (1869–1943)

## The Little Dancers

Lonely, save for a few faint stars, the sky
Dreams; and lonely, below, the little street
Into its gloom retires, secluded and shy.
Scarcely the dumb roar enters this soft retreat:
And all is dark, save where come flooding rays
From a tavern-window; there, to the brisk measure
Of an organ that down in an alley merrily plays,
Two children, all alone and no one by,
Holding their tattered frocks, thro' an airy maze
Of motion lightly threaded with nimble feet
Dance sedately; face to face they gaze,
Their eyes shining, grave with a perfect pleasure.

T. STURGE MOORE (1870–1944)

# Variation on Rimbaud's Prose-Poem Childhood

### I

This idol with black eyes and yellow hair,
Parentless, without court, and nobler far
In every land than gods in fables are,
Has azure and verdure insolently fair
For kingdom stretching forth till waves which bear
No vessels, breaking, name its shores by Fame's
Ferociously Greek, Slav, or Celtic names.
In forest-borders (dream's own blossoms there
Like bells chime softly till they, opening, shine)
Is the girl orange-lipped, her knees she yields
Doubled to clear floods welling o'er the fields,
Nakedness shadowed, flecked, and clothed in fine
By rainbow bands, the flora, and the sea:
Such innocence in such immensity!

### II

Ladies that there and back again still pace
On terraces close-neighbouring the sea,
Infantas, giantesses! Vert-de-gris,
A foam of verdure billows round the place;
Forbidding, proud, each woman-jewel's grace
Stands upright on rich soil in shrubbery
Or tiny garden's sun-nursed liberty . . .
Young mothers and grown sisters whose deep gaze
Far pilgrimages have with bygones filled,
Sultanas, princesses, tyrannical

In bearing and in costume how self-willed,
Little foreigners and folk amiable
Through mild unhappiness . . . last, boredom's part,
The chat's hour of 'dear body' and 'dear heart.'

## 'I met a seer'

I met a seer.
He held in his hands
The book of wisdom.
'Sir,' I addressed him,
'Let me read.'
'Child –' he began.
'Sir,' I said,
'Think not that I am a child,
For already I know much
Of that which you hold.
Aye, much.'

He smiled.
Then he opened the book
And held it before me. –
Strange that I should have grown so suddenly blind.

## Birches

When I see birches bend to left and right
Across the lines of straighter darker trees,
I like to think some boy's been swinging them.
But swinging doesn't bend them down to stay
As ice-storms do. Often you must have seen them
Loaded with ice a sunny winter morning
After a rain. They click upon themselves
As the breeze rises, and turn many-colored
As the stir cracks and crazes their enamel.
Soon the sun's warmth makes them shed crystal shells
Shattering and avalanching on the snow-crust –
Such heaps of broken glass to sweep away
You'd think the inner dome of heaven had fallen.
They are dragged to the withered bracken by the load,
And they seem not to break; though once they are bowed
So low for long, they never right themselves:
You may see their trunks arching in the woods
Years afterwards, trailing their leaves on the ground
Like girls on hands and knees that throw their hair
Before them over their heads to dry in the sun.
But I was going to say when Truth broke in
With all her matter-of-fact about the ice-storm
I should prefer to have some boy bend them
As he went out and in to fetch the cows –
Some boy too far from town to learn baseball,
Whose only play was what he found himself,
Summer or winter, and could play alone.
One by one he subdued his father's trees
By riding them down over and over again

Until he took the stiffness out of them,
And not one but hung limp, not one was left
For him to conquer. He learned all there was
To learn about not launching out too soon
And so not carrying the tree away
Clear to the ground. He always kept his poise
To the top branches, climbing carefully
With the same pains you use to fill a cup
Up to the brim, and even above the brim.
Then he flung outward, feet first, with a swish,
Kicking his way down through the air to the ground.
So was I once myself a swinger of birches.
And so I dream of going back to be.
It's when I'm weary of considerations,
And life is too much like a pathless wood
Where your face burns and tickles with the cobwebs
Broken across it, and one eye is weeping
From a twig's having lashed across it open.
I'd like to get away from earth awhile
And then come back to it and begin over.
May no fate wilfully misunderstand me
And half grant what I wish and snatch me away
Not to return. Earth's the right place for love:
I don't know where it's likely to go better.
I'd like to go by climbing a birch tree,
And climb black branches up a snow-white trunk
*Toward* heaven, till the tree could bear no more,
But dipped its top and set me down again.
That would be good both going and coming back.
One could do worse than be a swinger of birches.

## Before Summer Rain

Suddenly from all the green around you,
something – you don't know what – has disappeared;
you feel it creeping closer to the window,
in total silence. From the nearby wood

you hear the urgent whistling of a plover,
reminding you of someone's *Saint Jerome:*
so much solitude and passion come
from that one voice, whose fierce request the downpour

will grant. The walls, with their ancient portraits, glide
away from us, cautiously, as though
they weren't supposed to hear what we are saying.

And reflected on the faded tapestries now:
the chill, uncertain sunlight of those long
childhood hours when you were so afraid.

*translated from the German by Stephen Mitchell*

# Childhood

It would be good to give much thought, before
you try to find words for something so lost,
for those long childhood afternoons you knew
that vanished so completely – and why?

We're still reminded –: sometimes by a rain,
but we can no longer say what it means;
life was never again so filled with meeting,
with reunion and with passing on

as back then, when nothing happened to us
except what happens to things and creatures:
we lived their world as something human,
and became filled to the brim with figures.

And became as lonely as a sheperd
and as overburdened by vast distances,
and summoned and stirred as from far away,
and slowly, like a long new thread,
introduced into that picture-sequence
where now having to go on bewilders us.

*translated from the German by Edward Snow*

EDWARD THOMAS (1878–1917)

## Snow

In the gloom of whiteness,
In the great silence of snow,
A child was sighing
And bitterly saying: 'Oh,
They have killed a white bird up there on her nest,
The down is fluttering from her breast.'
And still it fell through that dusky brightness
On the child crying for the bird of the snow.

## Sympathetic Portrait of a Child

The murderer's little daughter
who is barely ten years old
jerks her shoulders
right and left
so as to catch a glimpse of me
without turning round.

Her skinny little arms
wrap themselves
this way then that
reversely about her body!
Nervously
she crushes her straw hat
about her eyes
and tilts her head
to deepen the shadow –
smiling excitedly!

As best as she can
she hides herself
in the full sunlight
her cordy legs writhing
beneath the little flowered dress
that leaves them bare
from mid-thigh to ankle –

Why has she chosen me
for the knife
that darts along her smile?

# Piano

Softly, in the dusk, a woman is singing to me:
Taking me back down the vista of years, till I see
A child sitting under the piano, in the boom of the tingling
  strings
And pressing the small, poised feet of a mother who smiles
  as she sings.

In spite of myself, the insidious mastery of song
Betrays me back, till the heart of me weeps to belong
To the old Sunday evenings at home, with winter outside
And hymns in the cosy parlour, the tinkling piano our
  guide.

So now it is vain for the singer to burst into clamour
With the great black piano appassionato. The glamour
Of childish days is upon me, my manhood is cast
Down in the flood of remembrance, I weep like a child for
  the past.

FRANCES CORNFORD (1886–1960)

# Childhood

I used to think that grown-up people chose
To have stiff backs and wrinkles round their nose,
And veins like small fat snakes on either hand,
On purpose to be grand.
Till through the banister I watched one day
My great-aunt Etty's friend who was going away,
And how her onyx beads had come unstrung.
I saw her grope to find them as they rolled;
And then I knew that she was helplessly old,
As I was helplessly young.

EDWIN MUIR (1887–1959)

# Childhood

Long time he lay upon the sunny hill,
  To his father's house below securely bound.
Far off the silent, changing sound was still,
  With the black islands lying thick around.

He saw each separate height, each vaguer hue,
  Where the massed islands rolled in mist away,
And though all ran together in his view
  He knew that unseen straits between them lay.

Often he wondered what new shores were there.
  In thought he saw the still light on the sand,
The shallow water clear in tranquil air,
  And walked through it in joy from strand to strand.

Over the sound a ship so slow would pass
  That in the black hill's gloom it seemed to lie.
The evening sound was smooth like sunken glass,
  And time seemed finished ere the ship passed by.

Gray tiny rocks slept round him where he lay,
  Moveless as they, more still as evening came,
The grasses threw straight shadows far away,
  And from the house his mother called his name.

JOHN CROWE RANSOM (1888–1974)

# Bells for John Whiteside's Daughter

There was such speed in her little body,
And such lightness in her footfall,
It is no wonder her brown study
Astonishes us all.

Her wars were bruited in our high window.
We looked among orchard trees and beyond
Where she took arms against her shadow,
Or harried unto the pond

The lazy geese, like a snow cloud
Dripping their snow on the green grass,
Tricking and stopping, sleepy and proud,
Who cried in goose, Alas,

For the tireless heart within the little
Lady with rod that made them rise
From their noon apple-dreams and scuttle
Goose-fashion under the skies!

But now go the bells, and we are ready,
In one house we are sternly stopped
To say we are vexed at her brown study,
Lying so primly propped.

# Animula

'Issues from the hand of God, the simple soul'
To a flat world of changing lights and noise,
To light, dark, dry or damp, chilly or warm;
Moving between the legs of tables and of chairs,
Rising or falling, grasping at kisses and toys,
Advancing boldly, sudden to take alarm,
Retreating to the corner of arm and knee,
Eager to be reassured, taking pleasure
In the fragrant brilliance of the Christmas tree,
Pleasure in the wind, the sunlight and the sea;
Studies the sunlit pattern on the floor
And running stags around a silver tray;
Confounds the actual and the fanciful,
Content with playing-cards and kings and queens,
What the fairies do and what the servants say.
The heavy burden of the growing soul
Perplexes and offends more, day by day;
Week by week, offends and perplexes more
With the imperatives of 'is and seems'
And may and may not, desire and control.
The pain of living and the drug of dreams
Curl up the small soul in the window seat
Behind the *Encyclopaedia Britannica*.
Issues from the hand of time the simple soul
Irresolute and selfish, misshapen, lame,
Unable to fare forward or retreat,
Fearing the warm reality, the offered good,
Denying the importunity of the blood,
Shadow of its own shadows, spectre in its own gloom,

Leaving disordered papers in a dusty room;
Living first in the silence after the viaticum.

Pray for Guiterriez, avid of speed and power,
For Boudin, blown to pieces,
For this one who made a great fortune,
And that one who went his own way.
Pray for Floret, by the boarhound slain between the yew
    trees,
Pray for us now and at the hour of our birth.

EDNA ST VINCENT MILLAY (1892–1950)

# Childhood is the Kingdom Where Nobody Dies

Childhood is not from birth to a certain age and at a certain
    age
The child is grown, and puts away childish things.
Childhood is the kingdom where nobody dies.

Nobody that matters, that is. Distant relatives of course
Die, whom one never has seen or has seen for an hour,
And they gave one candy in a pink-and-green striped bag,
    or a jack-knife
And went away, and cannot really be said to have lived
    at all.

And cats die. They lie on the floor and lash their tails,
And their reticent fur is suddenly all in motion
With fleas that one never knew were there,
Polished and brown, knowing all there is to know
Trekking off into the living world.
You fetch a shoe-box, but it's much too small, because she
    won't curl up now:
So you find a bigger box, and bury her in the yard, and
    weep.

But you do not wake up a month from then, two months,
A year from then, two years, in the middle of the night
And weep, with your knuckles in your mouth, and say Oh,
    God! Oh, God!
Childhood is the kingdom where nobody dies that matters,
    – mothers and fathers don't die.

And if you have said, 'For heaven's sake, must you always
    be kissing a person?'

Or, 'I do wish to gracious you'd stop tapping on the window
     with your thimble!'
Tomorrow, or even the day after tomorrow if you're busy
     having fun
Is plenty of time to say, 'I'm sorry, mother.'

To be grown up is to sit at the table with people who have
     died, who neither listen nor speak;
Who do not drink their tea, though they always said
Tea was such a comfort.

Run down into the cellar and bring up the last jar of
     raspberries; they are not tempted.
Flatter them, ask them what was it they said exactly
That time, to the bishop, or to the overseer, or to Mrs.
     Mason;
They are not taken in.
Shout at them, get red in the face, rise
Drag them up out of their chairs by their stiff shoulders and
     shake them and yell at them
They are not startled, they are not even embarrassed; they
     slide back into their chairs.

Your tea is cold now.
You drink it standing up,
And leave the house.

EDITH SODERGRAN (1892–1923)

# My Childhood Trees

My childhood trees stand tall in the grass
and shake their heads what has become of you?
Rows of pillars stand like reproaches: you're unworthy to
   walk beneath us!

You're a child and should know everything,
so why are you fettered by your illness?
You have become a human, alien and hateful.
As a child, you talked with us for hours,
your eyes were wise.
Now we would like to tell you the secret of your life:
the key to all secrets lies in the grass by the raspberry patch.

We want to shake you up, you sleeper,
we want to wake you, dead one, from your sleep.

*translated from the Finnish by Stina Katchadourian*

## Sonnet: To a Child

Sweet is your antique body, not yet young.
Beauty withheld from youth that looks for youth.
Fair only for your father. Dear among
Masters in art. To all men else uncouth
Save me; who know your smile comes very old,
Learnt of the happy dead that laughed with gods;
For earlier suns than ours have lent you gold,
Sly fauns and trees have given you jigs and nods.

But soon your heart, hot-beating like a bird's,
Shall slow down. Youth shall lop your hair,
And you must learn wry meanings in our words.
Your smile shall dull, because too keen aware;
And when for hopes your hand shall be uncurled,
Your eyes shall close, being open to the world.

# The Cool Web

Children are dumb to say how hot the day is,
How hot the scent is of the summer rose,
How dreadful the black wastes of evening sky.
How dreadful the tall soldiers drumming by.

But we have speech to chill the angry day,
And speech, to dull the rose's cruel scent.
We spell away the overhanging night,
We spell away the soldiers and the fright.

There's a cool web of language winds us in,
Retreat from too much joy or too much fear:
We grow sea-green at last and coldly die
In brininess and volubility.

But if we let our tongues lose self-possession,
Throwing off language and its watery clasp
Before our death, instead of when death comes,
Facing the wide glare of the children's day,
Facing the rose, the dark sky and the drums,
We shall go mad no doubt and die that way.

# Incident

Once riding in old Baltimore,
Heart-filled, head-filled with glee,
I saw a Baltimorean
Keep looking straight at me.

Now I was eight and very small,
And he was no whit bigger,
And so I smiled, but he poked out
His tongue, and called me, 'Nigger'.

I saw the whole of Baltimore
From May until December:
Of all the things that happened there
That's all that I remember

# Soap Suds

This brand of soap has the same smell as once in the big
House he visited when he was eight: the walls of the
    bathroom open
To reveal a lawn where a great yellow ball rolls back
    through a hoop
To rest at the head of a mallet held in the hands of a child.

And these were the joys of that house: a tower with a
    telescope;
Two great faded globes, one of the earth, one of the stars;
A stuffed black dog in the hall; a walled garden with bees;
A rabbit warren; a rockery; a vine under glass; the sea.

To which he has now returned. The day of course is fine
And a grown-up voice cries Play! The mallet slowly swings,
Then crack, a great gong booms from the dog-dark hall and
    the ball
Skims forward through the hoop and then through the next
    and then

Through hoops where no hoops were and each dissolves in
    turn
And the grass has grown head-high and an angry voice
    cries Play!
But the ball is lost and the mallet slipped long since from the
    hands
Under the running tap that are not the hands of a child.

E. J. SCOVELL (1907–99)

# Child Waking

The child sleeps in the daytime,
With his abandoned, with his jetsam look,
On the bare mattress, across the cot's corner;
Covers and toys thrown out, a routine labour.

Relaxed in sleep and light,
Face upwards, never so clear a prey to eyes;
Like a walled town, surprised out of the air
– All life called in, yet all laid bare

To the enemy above –
He has taken cover in daylight, gone to ground
In his own short length, his body strong in bleached
Blue cotton and his arms outstretched.

Now he opens eyes but not
To see at first; they reflect the light like snow
And I wait in doubt if he sleeps or wakes, till I see
Slight pain of effort at the boundary,

And hear how the trifling wound
Of bewilderment fetches a caverned cry
As he crosses out of sleep – at once to recover
His place and poise, and smile as I lift him over.

But I recall the blue-
White snowfield of his eyes empty of sight
High between dream and day, and think how there
The soul might rise visible as a flower.

## Child on Top of a Greenhouse

The wind billowing out the seat of my britches,
My feet crackling splinters of glass and dried putty,
The half-grown chrysanthemums staring up like accusers,
Up through the streaked glass, flashing with sunlight,
A few white clouds all rushing eastward,
A line of elms plunging and tossing like horses,
And everyone, everyone pointing up and shouting!

## In the Waiting Room

In Worcester, Massachusetts,
I went with Aunt Consuelo
to keep her dentist's appointment
and sat and waited for her
in the dentist's waiting room.
It was winter. It got dark
early. The waiting room
was full of grown-up people,
arctics and overcoats,
lamps and magazines.
My aunt was inside
what seemed like a long time
and while I waited I read
the *National Geographic*
(I could read) and carefully
studied the photographs:
the inside of a volcano,
black, and full of ashes;
then it was spilling over
in rivulets of fire.
Osa and Martin Johnson
dressed in riding breeches,
laced boots, and pith helmets.
A dead man slung on a pole
– 'Long Pig,' the caption said.
Babies with pointed heads
wound round and round with string;
black, naked women with necks
wound round and round with wire

like the necks of light bulbs.
Their breasts were horrifying.
I read it right straight through.
I was too shy to stop.
And then I looked at the cover:
the yellow margins, the date.
Suddenly, from inside,
came an *oh!* of pain
– Aunt Consuelo's voice –
not very loud or long.
I wasn't at all surprised;
even then I knew she was
a foolish, timid woman.
I might have been embarrassed,
but wasn't. What took me
completely by surprise
was that it was *me*:
my voice, in my mouth.
Without thinking at all
I was my foolish aunt,
I – we – were falling, falling,
our eyes glued to the cover
of the *National Geographic*,
February, 1918.

I said to myself: three days
and you'll be seven years old.
I was saying it to stop
the sensation of falling off
the round, turning world
into cold, blue-black space.
But I felt: you are an *I*,
you are an *Elizabeth*,

you are one of *them*.
*Why* should you be one, too?
I scarcely dared to look
to see what it was I was.
I gave a sidelong glance
– I couldn't look any higher –
at shadowy gray knees,
trousers and skirts and boots
and different pairs of hands
lying under the lamps.
I knew that nothing stranger
had ever happened, that nothing
stranger could ever happen.

Why should I be my aunt,
or me, or anyone?
What similarities –
boots, hands, the family voice
I felt in my throat, or even
the *National Geographic*
and those awful hanging breasts –
held us all together
or made us all just one?
How – I didn't know any
word for it – how 'unlikely' . . .
How had I come to be here,
like them, and overhear
a cry of pain that could have
got loud and worse but hadn't?

The waiting room was bright
and too hot. It was sliding
beneath a big black wave,
another, and another.

Then I was back in it.
The War was on. Outside,
in Worcester, Massachusetts,
were night and slush and cold,
and it was still the fifth
of February, 1918.

# First Death in Nova Scotia

In the cold, cold parlor
my mother laid out Arthur
beneath the chromographs:
Edward, Prince of Wales,
with Princess Alexandra,
and King George with Queen Mary.
Below them on the table
stood a stuffed loon
shot and stuffed by Uncle
Arthur, Arthur's father.

Since Uncle Arthur fired
a bullet into him,
he hadn't said a word.
He kept his own counsel
on his white, frozen lake,
the marble-topped table.
His breast was deep and white,
cold and caressable;
his eyes were red glass,
much to be desired.

'Come,' said my mother,
'Come and say good-bye
to your little cousin Arthur.'
I was lifted up and given
one lily of the valley
to put in Arthur's hand.
Arthur's coffin was
a little frosted cake,

and the red-eyed loon eyed it
from his white, frozen lake.

Arthur was very small.
He was all white, like a doll
that hadn't been painted yet.
Jack Frost had started to paint him
the way he always painted
the Maple Leaf (Forever).
He had just begun on his hair,
a few red strokes, and then
Jack Frost had dropped the brush
and left him white, forever.

The gracious royal couples
were warm in red and ermine;
their feet were well wrapped up
in the ladies' ermine trains.
They invited Arthur to be
the smallest page at court.
But how could Arthur go,
clutching his tiny lily,
with his eyes shut up so tight
and the roads deep in snow?

# Fern Hill

Now as I was young and easy under the apple boughs
About the lilting house and happy as the grass was green,
    The night above the dingle starry,
        Time let me hail and climb
    Golden in the heydays of his eyes,
And honoured among wagons I was prince of the apple
   towns
And once below a time I lordly had the trees and leaves
        Trail with daisies and barley
    Down the rivers of the windfall light.

And as I was green and carefree, famous among the barns
About the happy yard and singing as the farm was home,
    In the sun that is young once only,
        Time let me play and be
    Golden in the mercy of his means,
And green and golden I was huntsman and herdsman, the
   calves
Sang to my horn, the foxes on the hills barked clear and
   cold,
        And the sabbath rang slowly
    In the pebbles of the holy streams.

All the sun long it was running, it was lovely, the hay
Fields high as the house, the tunes from the chimneys, it
   was air
    And playing, lovely and watery
        And fire green as grass.
    And nightly under the simple stars
As I rode to sleep the owls were bearing the farm away,

All the moon long I heard, blessed among stables, the
    nightjars
        Flying with the ricks, and the horses
            Flashing into the dark.

And then to awake, and the farm, like a wanderer white
With the dew, come back, the cock on his shoulder: it was
    all
        Shining, it was Adam and maiden,
            The sky gathered again
        And the sun grew round that very day.
So it must have been after the birth of the simple light
In the first, spinning place, the spellbound horses walking
    warm
        Out of the whinnying green stable
            On to the fields of praise.

And honoured among foxes and pheasants by the gay
    house
Under the new made clouds and happy as the heart was
    long,
        In the sun born over and over,
            I ran my heedless ways,
        My wishes raced through the house high hay
And nothing I cared, at my sky blue trades, that time allows
In all his tuneful turning so few and such morning songs
        Before the children green and golden
            Follow him out of grace,

Nothing I cared, in the lamb white days, that time would
    take me
Up to the swallow thronged loft by the shadow of my hand,
        In the moon that is always rising,
            Nor that riding to sleep

[ 127 ]

I should hear him fly with the high fields
And wake to the farm forever fled from the childless land.
Oh as I was young and easy in the mercy of his means,
            Time held me green and dying
    Though I sang in my chains like the sea.

ROBERT HAYDEN (1913–80)

## Those Winter Sundays

Sundays too my father got up early
and put his clothes on in the blueblack cold,
then with cracked hands that ached
from labor in the weekday weather made
banked fires blaze. No one ever thanked him.

I'd wake and hear the cold splintering, breaking.
When the rooms were warm, he'd call,
and slowly I would rise and dress,
fearing the chronic angers of that house,

Speaking indifferently to him,
who had driven out the cold
and polished my good shoes as well.
What did I know, what did I know
of love's austere and lonely offices?

# A Young Child and His Pregnant Mother

At four years Nature is mountainous,
Mysterious, and submarine. Even

A city child knows this, hearing the subway's
Rumor underground. Between the grate,

Dropping his penny, he learned out all loss,
The irretrievable cent of fate,

And now this newest of the mysteries,
Confronts his honest and his studious eyes –

His mother much too fat and absentminded,
Gazing past his face, careless of him,

His fume, his charm, his bedtime, and warm milk,
As soon the night will be too dark, the spring

Too late, desire strange, and time too fast,
This estrangement is a gradual thing

(His mother once so svelte, so often sick!
Towering father did this: what a trick!)

Explained to cautiously, containing fear,
Another being's being, becoming dear:

All men are enemies: thus even brothers
Can separate each other from their mothers!

No better example than this unborn brother
Shall teach him of his exile from his mother,

Measured by his distance from the sky,
Spoken in two vowels,
I am I.

# A Sick Child

The postman comes when I am still in bed.
'Postman, what do you have for me today?'
I say to him. (But really I'm in bed.)
Then he says – what shall I have him say?

'This letter says that you are president
Of – this word here; it's a republic.'
Tell them I can't answer right away.
'It's your duty.' No, I'd rather just be sick.

Then he tells me there are letters saying everything
That I can think of that I want for them to say.
I say, 'Well, thank you very much. Good-bye.'
He is ashamed, and turns and walks away.

If I can think of it, it isn't what I want.
I want . . . I want a ship from some near star
To land in the yard, and beings to come out
And think to me: 'So this is where you are!

Come.' Except that they won't do,
I thought of them. . . . And yet somewhere there must be
Something that's different from everything.
All that I've never thought of – think of me!

# The Ball Poem

What is the boy now, who has lost his ball,
What, what is he to do? I saw it go
Merrily bouncing, down the street, and then
Merrily over – there it is in the water!
No use to say 'O there are other balls':
An ultimate shaking grief fixes the boy
As he stands rigid, trembling, staring down
All his young days into the harbour where
His ball went. I would not intrude on him,
A dime, another ball, is worthless. Now
He senses first responsibility
In a world of possessions. People will take balls,
Balls will be lost always, little boy,
And no one buys a ball back. Money is external.
He is learning, well behind his desperate eyes,
The epistemology of loss, how to stand up
Knowing what every man must one day know
And most know many days, how to stand up
And gradually light returns to the street,
A whistle blows, the ball is out of sight,
Soon part of me will explore the deep and dark
Floor of the harbour . . I am everywhere,
I suffer and move, my mind and my heart move
With all that move me, under the water
Or whistling, I am not a little boy.

# September, the First Day of School

### I

My child and I hold hands on the way to school,
And when I leave him at the first-grade door
He cries a little but is brave; he does
Let go. My selfish tears remind me how
I cried before that door a life ago.
I may have had a hard time letting go.

Each fall the children must endure together
What every child also endures alone:
Learning the alphabet, the integers,
Three dozen bits and pieces of a stuff
So arbitrary, so peremptory
That worlds invisible and visible

Bow down before it, as in Joseph's dream
The sheaves bowed down and then the stars bowed down
Before the dreaming of a little boy.
That dream got him such hatred of his brothers
As cost the greater part of life to mend,
And yet great kindness came of it in the end.

### II

A school is where they grind the grain of thought,
And grind the children who must mind the thought.
It may be those two grindings are but one,
As from the alphabet come Shakespeare's Plays,
As from the integers comes Euler's Law,
As from the whole, inseparably, the lives,

The shrunken lives that have not been set free
By law or by poetic phantasy.

But may they be. My child has disappeared
Behind the schoolroom door. And should I live
To see his coming forth, a life away,
I know my hope, but do not know its form

Nor hope to know it. May the fathers he finds
Among his teachers have a care of him
More than his father could. How that will look
I do not know, I do not need to know.
Even our tears belong to ritual.
But may great kindness come of it in the end.

## Boy at the Window

Seeing the snowman standing all alone
In dusk and cold is more than he can bear.
The small boy weeps to hear the wind prepare
A night of gnashings and enormous moan.
His tearful sight can hardly reach to where
The pale-faced figure with bitumen eyes
Returns him such a god-forsaken stare
As outcast Adam gave to Paradise.

The man of snow is, nonetheless, content,
Having no wish to go inside and die.
Still, he is moved to see the youngster cry.
Though frozen water is his element,
He melts enough to drop from one soft eye
A trickle of the purest rain, a tear
For the child at the bright pane surrounded by
Such warmth, such light, such love, and so much fear.

# Lot's Wife

How simple the pleasures of those childhood days,
Simple but filled with exquisite satisfactions.
The iridescent labyrinth of the spider,
Its tethered tensor nest of polygons
Puffed by the breeze to a little bellying sail –
Merely observing this gave infinite pleasure.
The sound of rain. The gentle graphite veil
Of rain that makes of the world a steel engraving,
Full of soft fadings and faint distances.
The self-congratulations of a fly,
Rubbing its hands. The brown bicameral brain
Of a walnut. The smell of wax. The feel
Of sugar to the tongue: a delicious sand.
One understands immediately how Proust
Might cherish all such postage-stamp details.
Who can resist the charms of retrospection?

DONALD JUSTICE (1925–2004)

## On the Death of Friends in Childhood

We shall not ever meet them bearded in heaven,
Nor sunning themselves among the bald of hell;
If anywhere, in the deserted schoolyard at twilight,
Forming a ring, perhaps, or joining hands
In games whose very names we have forgotten.
Come, memory, let us seek them there in the shadows.

## To Waken a Small Person

You sleep at the top of streets
Up which workmen each morning
Go wheeling their bicycles

Your eyes are like the windows
Of some high attic the one
The very one you sleep in

They're shut it's raining the rain
Falls on the streets of the town
As it falls through your sleep stop

You must be dreaming these tears
Wake up please open yourself
Like a little umbrella

Hurry the sidewalks need you
The awnings not one is up
And the patient bicycles

Halted at intersections
They need you they are confused
The colors of traffic lights

Are bleeding bleeding wake up
The puddles of parking lots
Cannot contain such rainbows

JAMES MERRILL (1926–95)

## The World and the Child

Letting his wisdom be the whole of love,
The father tiptoes out, backwards. A gleam
Falls on the child awake and wearied of,

Then, as the door clicks shut, is snuffed. The glove-
Gray afterglow appalls him. It would seem
That letting wisdom be the whole of love

Were pastime even for the bitter grove
Outside, whose owl's white hoot of disesteem
Falls on the child awake and wearied of.

He lies awake in pain, he does not move,
He will not call. The women, hearing him,
Would let their wisdom be the whole of love.

People have filled the room he lies above.
Their talk, mild variation, chilling theme,
Falls on the child. Awake and wearied of

Mere pain, mere wisdom also, he would have
All the world waking from its winter dream,
Letting its wisdom be. The whole of love
Falls on the child awake and wearied of.

ELIZABETH JENNINGS (1926–2001)

## A Child in the Night

The child stares at the stars. He does not know
Their names. He does not care. Time halts for him
And he is standing on the earth's far rim
As all the sky surrenders its bright show.

He will not feel like this again until
He falls in love. He will not be possessed
By dispossession till he has caressed
A face and in its eyes seen stars stand still.

# Full Moon and Little Frieda

A cool small evening shrunk to a dog bark and the clank of
    a bucket –

And you listening.
A spider's web, tense for the dew's touch.
A pail lifted, still and brimming – mirror
To tempt a first star to a tremor.

Cows are going home in the lane there, looping the hedges
    with their warm wreaths of breath –
A dark river of blood, many boulders,
Balancing unspilled milk.

'Moon!' you cry suddenly, 'Moon! Moon!'

The moon has stepped back like an artist gazing amazed at
    a work

That points at him amazed.

TONY CONNOR (1930–  )

## A Child Half-Asleep

Stealthily parting the small-hours silence,
a hardly-embodied figment of his brain
comes down to sit with me
as I work late.
Flat-footed, as though his legs and feet
were still asleep.

He sits on a stool,
staring into the fire,
his dummy dangling.

Fire ignites the small coals of his eyes.
It stares back through the holes
into his head, into the darkness.

I ask what woke him?

'A wolf dreamed me' he says.

## from *Mercian Hymns*

VI

The princes of Mercia were badger and raven. Thrall to
    their freedom. I dug and hoarded. Orchards fruited above
    clefts. I drank from honeycombs of chill sandstone.

'A boy at odds in the house, lonely among brothers.' But I,
    who had none, fostered a strangeness; gave myself to
    unattainable toys.

Candles of gnarled resin, apple-branches, the tacky
    mistletoe. 'Look' they said and again 'look'. But I ran
    slowly; the landscape flowed away, back to its source.

In the schoolyard, in the cloakrooms, the children boasted
    their scars of dried snot; wrists and knees garnished with
    impetigo.

VII

Gasholders, russet among fields. Milldams, marlpools that
    lay unstirring. Eel-swarms. Coagulations of frogs: once,
    with branches and half-bricks, he battered a ditchful;
    then sidled away from the stillness and silence.

Ceolred was his friend and remained so, even after the day
    of the lost fighter: a biplane, already obsolete and
    irreplaceable, two inches of heavy snub silver. Ceolred let
    it spin through a hole in the classroom-floorboards, softly,
    into the rat-droppings and coins.

After school he lured Ceolred, who was sniggering with
    fright, down to the old quarries, and flayed him. Then,
    leaving Ceolred, he journeyed for hours, calm and alone,
    in his private derelict sandlorry named *Albion*.

# Morning Song

Love set you going like a fat gold watch.
The midwife slapped your footsoles, and your bald cry
Took its place among the elements.

Our voices echo, magnifying your arrival. New statue.
In a drafty museum, your nakedness
Shadows our safety. We stand round blankly as walls.

I'm no more your mother
Than the cloud that distills a mirror to reflect its own slow
Effacement at the wind's hand.

All night your moth-breath
Flickers among the flat pink roses. I wake to listen:
A far sea moves in my ear.

One cry, and I stumble from bed, cow-heavy and floral
In my Victorian nightgown.
Your mouth opens clean as a cat's. The window square

Whitens and swallows its dull stars. And now you try
Your handful of notes;
The clear vowels rise like balloons.

## The Lesson

'Your father's gone,' my bald headmaster said.
His shiny dome and brown tobacco jar
Splintered at once in tears. It wasn't grief.
I cried for knowledge which was bitterer
Than any grief. For there and then I knew
That grief has uses – that a father dead
Could bind the bully's fist a week or two;
And then I cried for shame, then for relief.

I was a month past ten when I learnt this:
I still remember how the noise was stilled
In school-assembly when my grief came in.
Some goldfish in a bowl quietly sculled
Around their shining prison on its shelf.
They were indifferent. All the other eyes
Were turned towards me. Somewhere in myself
Pride, like a goldfish, flashed a sudden fin.

# Waking Jed

Deep asleep, perfect immobility, no apparent evidence of
   consciousness or of dream.
Elbow cocked, fist on pillow lightly curled to the tension of
   the partially relaxing sinew.
Head angled off, just so: the jaw's projection exaggerated
   slightly, almost to prognathous: why?
The features express nothing whatsoever and seem to call
   up no response in me.
Though I say nothing, don't move, gradually, far down
   within, he, or rather not *he* yet,
something, a presence, an element of being, becomes aware
   of me: there begins a subtle,
very gentle alteration in the structure of the face, or maybe
   less than that, more elusive,
as though the soft distortions of sleep-warmth radiating
   from his face and flesh,
those essentially unreal mirages in the air between us, were
   modifying, dissipating.
The face is now more his, Jed's – its participation in the
   almost Romanesque generality
I wouldn't a moment ago have been quite able to specify,
   not having its contrary, diminishes.
Particularly on the cheekbones and chin, the skin is
   thinning, growing denser, harder,
the molecules on the points of bone coming to attention,
   the eyelids finer, brighter, foil-like:
capillaries, veins; though nothing moves, there are goings
   to and fro behind now.

One hand opens, closes down more tightly, the arm extends
    suddenly full length,
jerks once at the end, again, holds: there's a more
    pronounced elongation of the skull –
the infant pudginess, whatever atavism it represented, or
    reversion, has been called back.
Now I sense, although I can't say how, his awareness of me:
    I can feel him begin to *think*,
I even know that he's thinking – or thinking in a dream
    perhaps – of me here watching him.
Now I'm aware – again, with no notion how, nothing
    indicates it – that if there was a dream,
it's gone, and, yes, his eyes abruptly open although his gaze,
    straight before him,
seems not to register just yet, the mental operations still
    independent of his vision.
I say his name, the way we do it, softly, calling one another
    from a cove or cave,
as though something else were there with us, not to be
    disturbed, to be crept along beside.
The lids come down again, he yawns, widely, very
    consciously manifesting intentionality.
Great, if rudimentary, pleasure now: a sort of primitive,
    peculiarly mammalian luxury –
to know, to know wonderfully that lying here, warm,
    protected, eyes closed, one can,
for a moment anyway, a precious instant, put off the lower
    specie onsets, duties, debts.
Sleeker, somehow, slyer, more aggressive now, he is
    suddenly more awake, all awake,
already plotting, scheming, fending off: nothing said but
    there is mild rebellion, conflict:

I insist, he resists, and then, with abrupt, wriggling grace,
   he otters down from sight,
just his brow and crown, his shining rumpled hair, left
   ineptly showing from the sheet.
Which I pull back to find him in what he must believe a
   parody of sleep, himself asleep:
fetal, rigid, his arms clamped to his sides, eyes screwed shut,
   mouth clenched, grinning.

## Being the Third Song of Urias

Lives ago, years past generations
perhaps nowhere I dreamed it:
the foggy ploughland of wind
and hoofprints, my father
off in the mist topping beats.

Where I was eight, I knew nothing,
the world a cold winter light
on half a dozen fields, then
all the winking blether of stars.

Before like a fool I began
explaining the key in its lost locked box
adding words to the words to the sum
that never works out.

           Where I was
distracted again by the lapwing,
the damp morning air of my father's
gregarious plainchant cursing
all that his masters deserved
and had paid for.
          Sure I was
then for the world's mere being
in the white rime on weeds
among the wet hawthorn berries
at the field's edge darkened by frost,
and none of these damned words to say it.

I began trailing out there in voices,
friends, women, my children,
my father's tetherless anger, some
like him who are dead who are
part of the rain now.

SEAMUS HEANEY (1939–   )

# The Railway Children

When we climbed the slopes of the cutting
We were eye-level with the white cups
Of the telegraph poles and the sizzling wires.

Like lovely freehand they curved for miles
East and miles west beyond us, sagging
Under their burden of swallows.

We were small and thought we knew nothing
Worth knowing. We thought words travelled the wires
In the shiny pouches of raindrops,

Each one seeded full with the light
Of the sky, the gleam of the lines, and ourselves
So infinitesimally scaled

We could stream through the eye of a needle.

# The Sunburst

Her first memory is of light all around her
As she sits among pillows on a patchwork quilt
Made out of uniforms, coat linings, petticoats,
Waistcoats, flannel shirts, ball gowns, by Mother
Or grandmother, twenty stitches to every inch,
A flawless version of *World without End* or
*Cathedral Window* or a diamond pattern
that radiates from the smallest grey square
Until the sunburst fades into the calico.

ROBERT PINSKY (1940–   )

# Daughter

## I

She thinks about skeletons,
Admires their symmetry,
Responding with fear
To the implied movement
And the near-absence of expression.
In the museum
Of natural history
She pressed up close
To the smaller ones;
But shook, studying the tall
Scaffolding of dinosaurs
From the next room.
Back home, sitting in the john
With the door open
She claims to see, in a mirror
Down the dark hall, her own.

## II

At certain times, midway
In a meal, or feeling
The dried mucus of her nose,
She stares nowhere like a cat.
It is not quite the same
As the damp sensual trance
Of her thumb. It does not
Seem to be thought, nor
The deep stare of a cat
Concentrating on a noise
Or a smell. It is like a cat

Staring nowhere. When she comes
Out of it or is interrupted
A great emptiness flares,
Of profound privacy,
Like a good Christian's death.

### III

With people, she deals oddly.
Normally too savage for bribes,
She attaches herself
In the way of a feudal tenant
To a grandma, overweight,
Spendthrift. The vassal
Declares prices,
Then haggles for a while.
She watches the two
Parents as they watch her
Pleasing herself with cheap
Toys and half-eaten sweets.
Chattering as two equals,
Nicole who calls herself 'Mary'
And the woman nobody loves enough
Trot downtown for their perms.

### IV

Like most children
She paints firmly and well,
Somewhat like Henri Rousseau.
She and her friends paint
With a mild firmness
Of attention. Their great
Interest when they discuss
Paintings they have made
Seems partly affected:

A habit, maybe, grown
From the ineluctable
Deal that their kind make.
Is the painting also
Part of the deal? Often, she
Smears over her work, thick
Strokes, as for painting a wall.

v

She chats quietly
With a few cronies
On the subject of death.
They all have something to say,
Her contribution being
To list her close family
In correct order of age,
Declaring that we will die
In the same order. Nobody
Disagrees. *I know it*,
They say, *I know it*. One
Tells about graves. And then
They drift off the subject
Like that many businesslike
Starlings, flying away
From one tree among trees.

HUGO WILLIAMS (1942– )

## Sugar Daddy

You do not look like me. I'm glad
England failed to colonize
Those black orchid eyes
With blue, the colour of sun-blindness.

Your eyes came straight to you
From your mother's Martinique
Great-grandmother. They look at me
Across this wide Atlantic

With an inborn feeling for my weaknesses.
Like loveletters, your little phoney grins
Come always just too late
To reward my passionate clowning.

I am here to be nice, clap hands, reflect
Your tolerance. I know what I'm for.
When you come home fifteen years from now
Saying you've smashed my car,

I'll feel the same. I'm blood brother,
Sugar daddy, millionaire to you.
I want to buy you things.

I bought a garish humming top
And climbed into your pen like an ape
And pumped it till it screeched for you,
Hungry for thanks. Your lip

Trembled and you cried. You didn't need
My sinister grenade, something
Pushed out of focus at you, swaying
Violently. You owned it anyway

[ 156 ]

And the whole world it came from.
It was then I knew
I could only take things from you from now on.

I was the White Hunter,
Bearing cheap mirrors for the Chief.
You saw the giving-look coagulate in my eyes
And panicked for the trees.

# The Unjustly Punished Child

The child screams in his room. Rage
heats his head.
He is going through changes like metal under deep
pressure at high temperatures.

When he cools off and comes out of that door
he will not be the same child who ran in
and slammed it. An alloy has been added. Now he will
crack along different lines when tapped.

He is stronger. The long impurification
has begun this morning.

# Five-Year-Old Boy

My son at five is leaning on the world
the way a factory foreman leans on
a slow worker. As he talks, he holds
a kitchen strainer in his hand. At the end of
the conversation, the handle is twisted,
the mesh burst – he looks down at it
amazed. Mysterious things are always
happening in his hands. As he tells a story,
he dances backwards. Nothing is safe
near this boy. He stands on the porch, peeing
into the grass, watching a bird
fly around the house, and ends up
pissing on the front door. Afterwards
he twangs his penis. Long after
the last drops fly into the lawn,
he stands there gently rattling himself,
his face full of intelligence,
his white, curved forehead slightly
puckered in thought, his eyes clear,
gazing out over the pond,
his mouth firm and serious;
abstractedly he shakes himself
once more
and the house collapses
to the ground behind him.

# Bran

While he looks into the eyes of women
Who have let themselves go,
While they sigh and they moan
For pure joy,

He weeps for the boy on that small farm
Who takes an oatmeal Labrador
In his arms,
Who knows all there is of rapture.

JOHN BURNSIDE (1955–   )

# Occasional Poem
*Charity Graepel, aged 2 months*

Before the words for things
arrive in her mind,
there is only a sequence of echoes:
the wet eyes and rust-coloured hair,
the angle and pivot of bone
in the loose dark skin –

and she lives in a different state, where we
are fluid and indistinct,
figments of sound and nurture
flaring, then burning out,

and what she knows of dogs, or light,
or water, is a mystery to us,
who have them named and lost, a truth resolved
in the grammar that clothes and undermines our thought,
and shadows her wonder at this, the impossible world.

# Homesick

When we love, when we tell ourselves we do,
we are pining for first love, somewhen,
before we thought of wanting it. When we rearrange
the rooms we end up living in, we are looking
for first light, the arrangement of light,
that time, before we knew to call it light.

Or talk of music, when we say
we cannot talk of it, but play again
C major, A flat minor, we are straining
for first sound, what we heard once,
then, in lost chords, wordless languages.

What country do we come from? This one?
The one where the sun burns
when we have night? The one
the moon chills; elsewhere, possible?

Why is our love imperfect,
music only echo of itself,
the light wrong?

We scratch in dust with sticks,
dying of homesickness
for when, where, what.

KATE CLANCHY (1967–  )

## Mitigation

We think you know the secret places,
the ones you called, perhaps, *Big Sands*,
*The Den*, or *Grassy Hill*. They loom up large
behind your eyes. Those hands that stroke
your signet ring, were once, like ours, blunt-
fingered, small, and clutched at grass or clenched
a stone and loved the tender, ticking throat

of panicked bird or retching child.
You watched the films, played Dracula.
That doll was yours whose head came off.
You stored her up behind the fort, the patch
of dirt around her mouth. There's something
buried in the park, a shallow grave, a rotting
thrush. You know the place. And know

the swooping railway tracks and why
we stole a child, like sweeties, from the shops.
You twitch and feel the small wet thrill.
You balked, you bottled, ran, that's all.
We heard you from the Policeman's van.
We heard your hands, the short, sharp slaps
of grown-ups clamouring to get back.

# Acknowledgements

The editor and publishers gratefully acknowledge permission to reprint copyright material in the this book as follows, and would be pleased to hear from any untraced copyright holders who will be acknowledged in future editions of this book: JOHN BERRYMAN: 'The Ball Poem', from *The Dispossessed* (1948); *Collected Poems 1937–1971* (Faber, 1991). LAURENCE BINYON: 'The Little Dancers' © The Society of Authors as the Literary Representative of the Estate of Laurence Binyon. ELIZABETH BISHOP: 'First Death in Nova Scotia' and 'In the Waiting Room', from *The Complete Poems: 1927–1979* by Elizabeth Bishop. Copyright © 1979, 1983 by Alice Helen Methfessel. Reprinted by permission of Farrar, Straus and Giroux LLC. JOHN BURNSIDE: 'Occasional Poem', from *The Myth Of The Twin*, published by Jonathan Cape. Reprinted by permission of The Random House Group Ltd. KATE CLANCHY: 'Mitigation', from *Slattern* (Chatto, 1995; Picador, 2001). TONY CONNOR: 'A Child Half-Asleep', from *Tony Connor: New and Selected Poems*, published by Anvil Press Poetry in 1982. COUNTEE CULLEN: 'Incident', from *On These I Stand* (New York: Harper, 1925). Copyright © 1925 by Harper & Brothers, renewed 1953 by Ida M. Cullen. Reprinted by permission of GRM Associates Inc., Agents for the Estate of Ida M. Cullen. EMILY DICKINSON: 'From all the Jails the Boys and Girls' and 'The Child's faith is new', reprinted by permission of the publishers and the Trustees of Amherst College from *The Poems of Emily Dickinson*, Thomas H. Johnson ed., Cambridge Mass: The Belknap Press of Harvard University Press, Copyright © 1951, 1955, 1979, 1983 by the President and Fellows of Harvard College. CAROL ANN DUFFY: 'Homesick' is taken from *Selling Manhattan* by Carol Ann Duffy published by Anvil Press Poetry in 1987. T. S. ELIOT: 'Animula', from *Collected Poems 1909–1962* (Faber, 1963). ROBERT FROST: 'Birches', from *The Poetry of Robert Frost*, edited by Edward Connery Latham, published by Jonathan Cape. Reprinted by permission of The Random House Group Ltd. ROBERT GRAVES: 'The Cool Web', from *Selected Poems* (Penguin, 1986). ROBERT HAYDEN: 'Those Winter Sundays', Copyright © 1966 Robert Hayden, from *Angle Of Ascent: New And Selected Poems* by Robert Hayden. Used by permission of

edited by Edmund Blunden, published by Chatto & Windus. Reprinted by permission of The Random House Group Ltd. ROBERT PINSKY: 'Daughter', from *The Figured Wheel* (Carcanet, 1996). Used by permission of Carcanet Press. SYLVIA PLATH: 'Morning Song', from *Ariel* (Faber, 1965); *Collected Poems* (Faber, 1981). John Crowe Ransom: 'Bells for John Whiteside's Daughter', from *Selected Poems* (Alfred A. Knopf 1969 And Carcanet 1991). RAINER MARIA RILKE: 'Before Summer Rain', copyright © 1982 by Stephen Mitchell, from *The Selected Poetry of Rainer Maria Rilke*, by Rainer Maria Rilker, translated by Stephen Mitchell. Used by permission of Random House, Inc. THEODORE ROETHKE: 'Child on Top of a Greenhouse', from *The Lost Son and Other Poems* (1948); *Collected Poems* (1966; Faber, 1968, 1985). DELMORE SCHWARTZ: 'A Young Child and his Pregnant Mother', from *Selected Poems: Summer Knowledge*, copyright © 1954, 1955, 1958, 1959 by Delmore Schwartz, copyright © 1959 Modern Poetry Association, copyright © 1959 Harrison-Blaine, Inc. Reprinted by permission of New Directions Publishing Corp. E. J. SCOVELL: 'Child Waking', from *Collected Poems* (Carcanet, 1988). Used by permission of Carcanet Press. KEN SMITH: 'Being the Third Song of Urias', *The Poet Reclining: Selected Poems 1962–1980* (Bloodaxe Books, 1982). EDITH SODERGRAN: 'My Childhood Trees', trans. Stina Katchadourian, from *Love and Solitude: selected poems of Edith Sodergran* (Fjord Press, 1996). DYLAN THOMAS: 'Fern Hill', from *The Collected Poems of Dylan Thomas 1934–1953* (Dent, 1996). EDWARD THOMAS: 'Snow', from *Collected Poems* (Faber & Faber, 2004). HENRY VAUGHAN, 'Childhood' and 'The Retreat', from *Henry Vaughan: The Complete Poems*, edited by Alan Rudrum (Penguin Classics, 1995). RICHARD WILBUR: 'Boy at The Window', from *New and Collected Poems* (Faber, 1989). ALEXANDER DER WILDE: to University of Chicago Press, 'When We Were Children', trans. © David Ferry, from *Dwelling Places* (University of Chicago Press, 1993). C. K. WILLIAMS: 'Waking Jed', from *New and Selected Poems* (Bloodaxe Books, 1995). HUGO WILLIAMS: 'Sugar Daddy', from *Sugar Daddy*, 1970; *Collected Poems*, (Faber 2002). WILLIAM CARLOS WILLIAMS: 'Sympathetic Portrait of a Child' from *Al Que Quiere!*, in *Collected Poems* (Carcanet, 1987). Used by permission of Carcanet Press. W. B. YEATS: 'To a Child Dancing in the Wind', from *Collected Poems* (Picador, 1990).

# Index of Poets